T0330656

Truth in Marketing

Although highly philosophical in nature, this scholarly text is essential reading for senior marketing practitioners, researchers and students. I thought I knew what truth was until I read this book, and while your head will hurt when you read it, it will be good for the world of marketing if you do. In this case the journey through abstract philosophy has concrete implications for the way marketers design their practices. Highly recommended reading (and re-reading).

—*Linda Brennan, Professor in the School of Media and Communication, RMIT University, Australia*

Can we believe the claims that marketers make? Does truth in marketing matter? Apparently not ...

Despite the role of regulators, marketing claims are often ruled to be misleading, deceptive or incomplete. Surprisingly, scholars of marketing ethics have devoted little time to this key issue. This may be because although key codes of marketing conduct insist on truthful communications, there is only limited understanding of what truthfulness itself actually entails.

This innovative book develops a theory of truth in marketing and discusses the implications for consumers, marketing professionals and policymakers. Focusing on the problem of truth in marketing, it analyses the theory of truth in marketing, and examines the wider significance of marketing truth for society. Using a wide selection of engaging global examples and cases to illustrate this fascinating analysis, this engaging book will provide a provocative read for all scholars and educators in marketing, marketing/business ethics and CSR.

Thomas Boysen Anker is lecturer at the University of Glasgow and holds a PhD in applied philosophy from the University of Copenhagen. His main research interest is business ethics. He is associate editor of *European Management Journal* and has published widely in international academic journals.

Routledge Focus on Business and Management

The fields of business and management have grown exponentially as areas of research and education. This growth presents challenges for readers trying to keep up with the latest important insights. Routledge Focus on Business and Management presents small books on big topics and how they intersect with the world of business.

Individually, each title in the series provides coverage of a key academic topic, whilst collectively, the series forms a comprehensive collection across the business disciplines.

Careers and Talent Management
A critical perspective
Cristina Reis

Management Accounting for Beginners
Nicholas Apostolides

Truth in Marketing
A theory of claims evidence relations
Thomas Boysen Anker

A Short Guide to People Management
For HR and line managers
Antonios Panagiotakopoulous

Truth in Marketing

A theory of claim-evidence relations

Thomas Boysen Anker

Routledge
Taylor & Francis Group

LONDON AND NEW YORK

First published 2016
by Routledge
2 Park Square, Milton Park, Abingdon, Oxon OX14 4RN

and by Routledge
711 Third Avenue, New York, NY 10017

Routledge is an imprint of the Taylor & Francis Group, an informa business

© 2016 Thomas Boysen Anker

British Library Cataloguing in Publication Data
A catalogue record for this book is available from the British Library

Library of Congress Cataloging-in-Publication Data

Names: Anker, Thomas Boysen, author.
Title: Truth in marketing: a theory of claim-evidence relations / Thomas Boysen Anker.
Description: Abingdon, Oxon; New York, NY : Routledge, 2016. |
Series: Routledge studies in business ethics | Includes bibliographical references and index.
Identifiers: LCCN 2015049595| ISBN 9781138849198 (hardback) |
ISBN 9781315725796 (ebook)
Subjects: LCSH: Deceptive advertising. | Marketing—Moral and ethical aspects.
Classification: LCC HF5827.8 .A55 2016 | DDC 174/.4—dc23
LC record available at http://lccn.loc.gov/2015049595

ISBN: 978-1-138-84919-8 (hbk)
ISBN: 978-1-315-72579-6 (ebk)

Typeset in Times New Roman
by codeMantra

**To my wife
Charlotte
and our children
Samira, Sylvester, Leo and Aviaya**

—*For providing the creative chaos that made this
book possible ...*

Contents

Figures and tables

Figures

Tables

Acknowledgements

I would like to thank the editorial team at Routledge. In particular, I am grateful to Jacqueline Curthoys for believing in the manuscript from day one and to Sinead Waldron for all her help and encouragement throughout the entire process.

Thanks also to all my colleagues in the Marketing Research Cluster at the Adam Smith Business School, University of Glasgow, for providing vital feedback on the basic ideas that form the backbone of this book at a research seminar. I would also like to thank Sabina Siebert for reading parts of the manuscript and for always being there to discuss theoretical problems.

I have also benefited from the generous comments of the audience at the World Social Marketing Conference 2015, Sydney, Australia, where I presented a paper on truth in social marketing. That paper was co-authored by Linda Brennan and Dorthe Brogård Kristensen, to whom I am also thankful for comments, insights and ideas.

Special thanks to John Finch for pointing me in the direction of American pragmatism: more than anyone James, Peirce and Dewey became my strongest inspiration.

1 Specifying the domain

> We can talk of mind, matter, numbers, time, or of what was, or will be, or might have been, and we can talk of mundane things like snow and penguins. And on all these matters, we can say things that are true, or, of course, things that are not true. So what is truth, if propositions from any sphere of interest can equally share it?
>
> Simon Blackburn and Keith Simmons, *Truth*

1.1 The problem of truth in marketing

There is universal agreement that truthfulness should be a core principle of all types of marketing communications. One example of the unanimous commitment to truthfulness is the International Chamber of Commerce's (ICC) standards of good marketing practice, known as the ICC Code. Since its inception in 1937, the ICC Code has formed the cornerstone for marketing regulation around the globe and is now operating in 35 countries. Article 1 of the Basic Principles of the ICC Code (ICC 2011) states: "All marketing communications should be legal, decent, honest and truthful."

Truth in marketing is indisputably a fundamental principle endorsed by all key stakeholders. This observation immediately questions the relevance of this book: why endeavor to develop a theory of truth in marketing when truthfulness already enjoys a central role in marketing regulation?

On the one hand, it is blatantly obvious that truthfulness − or rather the lack thereof − is a significant problem in marketing practice. One of the most telling recent examples is the VW emission scandal. The carmaker fitted vehicles with defeat devices that could identify test conditions and reduce engine capacity during tests and thereby systematically manipulated emission test results for millions of cars. Greenpeace protesters underlined the problem with graphical clarity: demonstrating outside the German headquarters in September 2015, they were carrying signs with the VW logo and the caption "No More Lies" ("Schluss mit Lügen"). It is beyond doubt that truth in marketing is a sizable moral problem. And it is not just an isolated problem correlated with the misconduct of individuals: the VW case demonstrates it to be a systemic problem that sometimes permeates entire multinational corporations. The temptation to deceive even seems to be endemic in that the entire car industry has a history of developing ingenious defeat devices, dating back to the 1970s (Plungis 2015). Yet, the moral problem of truth is not the aim of this book.

On the other hand, truthfulness is also a theoretical problem with substantial implications for marketing practice and regulation. This becomes evident upon analysis of the scope of the ICC Code's Article 1 quoted above: all marketing communications should be truthful. This sounds straightforward but is anything but: marketing communications comprise a vast range of different types of claims – functional, symbolic, experiential, behavioural – and to agree that these claims should be true is of little use unless one understands how these claims are made true. Are all marketing claims true in the same way? Should a claim like 'This salmon pate contains Omega 3 acid' be substantiated in the same way as a symbolic claim in a shampoo ad that associates the use of the product with sexual attractiveness? If yes, what concept of truth allows us to account for this broad range of radically different claims? If no, what different criteria of truth are applicable? These are tough questions, which marketing regulations do not answer. This alethic under-determination implies that the universal commitment to truth in marketing is to a large extent non-operational. This is the epistemological problem of truth in marketing, which this book addresses.

Accordingly, the aim of this exploration is to develop a theory of truth that defines what it is for different types of marketing claims to be true.

1.2   What is a theory of truth in marketing?

The opening section established the need for a theory of truth in marketing. But it did not address the underlying question as to what *type* of theory is in demand. To answer that question, it is useful to distinguish between two very broad types: propositional and sociological theories of truth.

Roughly, propositional theories hold that truth is analysable in terms of the content of a statement or belief, P, and P's relationship to the external world or the content of other statements or beliefs. Propositional theories of truth have been discussed since the dawn of Western philosophy. There are explicit discussions of propositional truth in both Plato (*Cratylos* 385b2; *Sophist* 263b) and Aristotle (*Metaphysics* 1011b25), and it continues to be a key topic in contemporary epistemology.[1] The aim of this book is to develop a propositional theory of truth in marketing. However, the concept of truth has been subject to intense critique in modern sociological theory. And this critique renders the development of a propositional theory of truth in marketing irrelevant. It is therefore necessary to justify the endeavour of this book.

Rather than the alethic function of statements and beliefs, it is the ideological manifestations of truth in contemporary society that is of interest to the sociological critique. In this context, Baudrillard's studies of the consumer society (1994, 1998) are particularly important. He argues that consumers live in a marketing-constructed reality of signs and symbols (simulacra) that have no reality and that, as a consequence, the notion of truth – in particular the notion of truth in marketing – is a superficial misnomer. Truth in marketing is an oxymoron because the societal function of marketing is to surround citizens with a persuasive narrative that produces the fundamental need to individualize through consumption. Marketing is the particular method of a certain type of societal system to generate the human needs that are necessary for the survival of the system (i.e., capitalism). This is the *truth about marketing*. To speak of truth *in marketing* is missing the point.[2]

Such sociological theories of the role of truth in social systems are relevant to the critique of the foundational premises of those systems. However, any given individual lives within a particular social system: from the internal point of view the external critique of the system may be ideologically relevant, but it has little practical relevance. What makes a *true* difference is the particular rules of the system that guide, shape and regulate actions within the broad parameters of the system's cornerstone assumptions.

A propositional theory of truth in marketing is relevant because our actions vis-à-vis consumers are hugely important to us. When brands lie or mislead us, it often has serious implications. To reiterate just one example from the introduction: VW's decision to fit its cars with devices that rig the tests of exhaust emissions has had profound practical implications: customers suffer financial losses (e.g., depreciation of the value of their cars); public trust in brands, which is crucial to the functioning of liberal societies, is undermined; the company itself is facing multibillion fines and has consequently posted its first losses in more than 15 years, with serious implications for employees and suppliers. Lying to customers hurts.

Surprisingly, studies of truth in marketing conducted from the internal point of view as opposed to the external meta-critique of the ideological function of truth in capitalistic society, has received very little attention. Apart from introductory remarks (e.g., Spence and van Heekeren 2005), there has been no conceptual analysis of truth in marketing in terms of claim–evidence relations.[3] This book pioneers the research area by developing a set of alethic criteria specifically designed to evaluate the veracity of propositional claims in marketing. The exploration draws heavily on three propositional theories developed within analytic philosophy: the correspondence, coherence and instrumental theories of truth. Before introducing these theories in the next three chapters, it is necessary to define the basic terminology used throughout the book.

1.3 Constructs of meaning

Marketing expressions and entities

Marketing expressions are theoretical constructs. They are composite units of complex meaning, which synthezise subordinate sets of meaning (claims and propositions) into one brand narrative. They communicate the entirety of meaning associated with a brand, product or service.

A marketing entity is any material or immaterial component of a deliberate marketing effort aimed at a target audience. Expressions are constituted by one or more marketing entities such as an ad, a series of ad or an integrated campaign spanning various channels (social media, print, broadcast, etc.)

Marketing entities are distributed temporally across the context of enquiry: a truth investigation may be limited to a specific point in time such as the truthfulness of a specific billboard ad. Or it may span various time-sections such as a truth investigation into a social media campaign, which encourages consumers to interact with the brand over time. Marketing entities also possess spatial properties: they may be spatially fixed like a one-off sponsorship of a sports event, or spatially distributed via integration of various channels (social media, print, broadcast) cutting across the physical/digital divide and taking place at various locations across the globe. It is the aim and extent of the truth investigation that determines the nature and scope of the marketing entities to be included for analysis.

Accordingly, let a marketing expression be the totality of meaning associated with a brand, product or service, which is conveyed by one or more marketing entities within a specified spatiotemporal domain by means of one or more sets of claims and propositions.

Claims and propositions

A claim makes a *general* assertion that something is or will be the case, whereas a proposition makes a *particular* assertion that something is or will be the case. For the purposes of this exploration, the domain of marketing comprises three different types of claims and propositions: functional, symbolic and behavioural.[4]

Functional claims and propositions state or imply that a product or service has certain properties and that consumption or use of the product or service satisfies a specific consumer need (Bhat and Reddy 1998; Guo, Wei Hao, and Shang 2011; Orth and De Marchi 2007; Park, Jaworski, and MacInnis 1986). For example, Colgate toothpaste claims 'Cavity protection' and 'Contains fluoride' and makes the implicit suggestion that it 'Strengthens the tooth enamel.' These are clear-cut functional claims and propositions. Functional needs may be simple (such as the need for cavity protection) or very complex (for example, how to analyze big data sets).

Functional properties may be material ('this watch is water resistant to 50 atm') or immaterial (a consultancy promising to increase your business's profitability).

Symbolic claims and propositions state or imply that using a specific product or service will associate the consumer with desirable social values (Bhat and Reddy 1998; Lee 2013; Park, Jaworski, and MacInnis 1986). Symbolic claims and propositions thereby address a wide range of psychological and emotional needs. For example, research in the field of consumer culture theory (Annamma and Li 2012; Arnould and Thompson 2005; Schembri, Merrilees, and Kristiansen 2010) demonstrates how consumers use brands as narrative material to construct and express self-identity and signal group belonging. Think of Apple's iconic iPod ads featuring silhouettes – black against a yellow, green, red or blue monochrome background – of young people dancing by themselves with iPods in their hands. These ads clearly associate the product with symbolic values of self-confident self-expression and aim at influencing the target audience to associate with the lifestyle values expressed in the ads.

Traditionally, the distinction between different types of marketing claims also includes experiential claims (Park, Jaworski, and MacInnis 1986). There are two reasons why the theory of truth in marketing operates with the notion of *behavioural* claims and propositions rather than *experiential*. First, Park, Jaworski and MacInnis (1986) define experiential claims in terms of consumer needs for sensory and cognitive stimulation. These needs are clearly different from functional needs, such as the need for waterproof clothing when walking in the hills on a rainy day. Yet, sensory and cognitive stimulation are to a large extent product dependent: an ice cream tastes delicious because of the composition of ingredients; a movie is exciting because it has a gripping storyline; reading the *Financial Times* provides cognitive stimulation (to some, at least) because the articles are well researched. In these examples, the experiential benefits are driven by the functional properties of the products. In terms of truth evaluations, experiential claims seem reducible to some type of functional claim and thereby do not manifest as a separate category.

Second, the traditional distinction between functional, symbolic and experiential cannot accommodate the behavioural dimension of many brand expressions. As Anker et al. (2012, 2015) point out, some marketing claims have a strong behavioural component, meaning that the brand can only deliver on its promise insofar as the consumer engages with the brand and adopts certain courses of action as specified by the brand. This is, for example, the case with health brands (like Kellogg's Special K) that claim to help consumers to lead a healthy lifestyle. Consumption of a given product cannot make a consumer healthy, as food-related health is a complex function of a varied diet. Health brands that make general claims about improving or maintaining health therefore have to engage consumers in wider, health-conducive courses of actions (Anker et al. 2011).

Behavioural claims of this sort are normal encounters in the marketplace. For example, brands that promise to facilitate creativity (Apple), enhance physical performance (Nike, Adidas, Puma, Lucozade), or improve the bases of self-esteem (Dove) all rely heavily on the consumer to deliver their promises. A new laptop crammed with specs that allow you to work creatively with photos and videos does not make you creative: it facilitates creativity insofar as you as the consumer decide to adopt certain courses of action, that is, to use the software in particular ways devised by your own ideas and shaped by your own capabilities and effort (Anker et al. 2012). Performance-enhancing products may actually enhance performances but only under certain narrowly defined circumstances such as vigorous exercise or mountaineering. You as the consumer need to adopt certain extended courses of actions, bringing the product into a context where it can deliver its promise.

Against this background, behavioural claims and propositions state or imply that a product or service will allow a given state of affairs to obtain if the consumer adopts a specific course of action, as indicated by the brand narrative when using the product or service.

Non-verbal claims and propositions

Section 1.2. introduced the distinction between propositional and non-propositional theories of truth and argued why there is a need for a propositional theory of truth in marketing. Traditionally, propositional theories of truth and meaning have been applied to content that can be stated in concise declarative sentences. This is natural in the sense that those studying these topics have predominantly been occupied with verbal claims and statements as well as propositional attitudes (e.g., beliefs), which can be formulated in natural or formal languages (e.g., symbolic logic). Discussions of propositional truth have therefore disregarded visual and symbolic meaning (Groarke 2013). This may fuel the objection that a theory of propositional truth in marketing is limited to written communications, say in advertising, on social media and in product descriptions.

However, visuals often convey claims and propositions. Birdsell and Groarke (2007) argue that traditional accounts of meaning have impeded the understanding of the complex function of visuals in rational discourse because imagery has been seen to convey emotions rather than cognitions. Developments in the field of visual argumentation demonstrate that visuals fulfil a raft of cognitive functions (Blair 2012). For example, Groarke and Tindale's (2012) typology of visual meaning clarifies that visuals often make propositional claims: maps are visual – but very exact – representations of a piece of land, expressing propositions about the physical shape of a landscape; road signs communicate simple but forceful propositions about how people in traffic must behave; graphs and flowcharts aid the formation of propositional understanding by simplifying complex data sets. Claims and propositions are thereby not restricted to verbal discourse. Consequently, all aspects of marketing may play an active role in conveying meaning to customers and consumers.

1.4 Domain epistemology

Expressions, claims and propositions all play different roles in the evaluation of truth in marketing. Expressions and claims are either true or false or have any degree of truth in between. They thereby possess truthlikeness or verisimilitude (Oddie 2014; Niiniluoto 1998). This means that they are truthful to a greater or lesser extent and that the theory of truth in marketing thereby operates within a truth-continuum.[5] The degree of verisimilitude that expressions possess is relative to the truth-values assigned to its claims. Truth-values, in turn, are ascribed to claims relative to the truth of their constituent propositions. Being the minimum unit of analysis, propositions act as *truth-bearers* and thereby refer to *truth-makers* that express the conditions under which propositions are true. The following subsections explain these core concepts in greater detail.

Verisimilitude

Popper (1963, 1976, 1979) developed the concept of verisimilitude. The basic idea is that a given scientific hypothesis or theory contains information that entails a series of logical consequences. These consequences are assessable in terms of truth or falsity. If two theories, T_1 and T_2, each comprise a set of true and false statements, but the set that belongs to T_1 contains more true statements than the set that belongs to T_2, then T_1 is closer to the truth than T_2 (Niiniluoto 1998). A theory is thereby not true or false in any absolute sense; it possesses a greater or lesser degree of truth or falsity relative to the truth-content or falsity-content of its compositional statements.

Verisimilitude powerfully captures common-sense intuitions about the nature of truth. For example, the claim 'The UN comprises 200 member states' is false, because the UN counts 193 member states. But at the same time the claim is closer to the truth than the competing claim 'The UN comprises 10.000 member states.'

It is also important to note another feature of the theory, which will strike many as counterintuitive. Popper advocates falsificationism, which is the view that it is possible to demonstrate scientific theories to be false but impossible to establish whether they are true. Popper dismantles the concept of truth in the sense that no theory can ever be proven to be true, but his notion of verisimilitude still allows for the concept of truth to be the driving force behind scientific discovery.

The theory of truth in marketing adopts two key insights from Popper. First, truth and falsity are defined in terms of subclass relationships (Popper

1968): it is the relationships between the truth- and falsity-content of individual propositions in sets of propositions as well as between different types of claims that establish the degree to which a marketing expression is true. Second, marketing expressions here take the place of scientific theories and may display a greater or lesser degree of truth (verisimilitude).

Contrary to Popper, the theory of truth in marketing does not operate from a falsificationist platform. Marketing truth investigations aim at establishing whether propositions are true or false. In cases where all relevant propositions and, consequently, all claims have been established to be true, the marketing expression is true. The world may never see any entirely true marketing expressions, but in theory this could be the case. Likewise, if a truth investigation finds all relevant propositions and, consequently, all claims to be false, the marketing expression is false. In most practical cases, however, the multitude of claims and propositions on which most brand universes are founded makes it reasonable to expect that one or more propositions will be false. Most marketing expressions and many claims may therefore be expected to have a given degree of truth (verisimilitude).[6]

The notion of verisimilitude is of great practical relevance because it allows for a detailed evaluation of different parts of marketing claims and expressions. A given brand, say a pharmaceutical brand for painkillers, may be found to be entirely consistent and true in terms of all factual claims. At the same time, truth interrogations may also establish the indicated pattern of normal consumption to be exaggerated and thereby not true. It has, for example, been documented that pharmaceutical marketing often medicalizes normal conditions in order to extend the target group and increase consumption of medication (Moynihan and Cassels 2005; Moynihan et al. 2002).

For the purposes of this exploration, we define verisimilitude as follows: For any given marketing expression, P, there is a subset of meaningful claims and propositions, which ascribe a degree of truth to P, ranging from absolute true to absolute false and allowing any degree of truth in between.

Truth-bearers

Propositions are the minimum unit of truth analysis. They carry truth content against which all other interpretations of truthfulness will be based and are therefore called truth-bearers (Glanzberg 2014; MacBride 2014). In contrast to expressions and claims, propositions are either true or false. This non-relative notion of propositional truth is a necessary component, in order to avoid epistemic regress problems. It is also a controversial component and so needs some explanation and justification.

It is a foundational assumption of the theory that truth evaluations of marketing claims or promises have to start with establishing the binary truth or falsity of propositions. It is necessary to introduce this non-relative function of truth in order to operationalize the theory and enable the evaluation of actual marketing claims and promises in theoretical and practical contexts. If all truth functions were relative to some other truth function, then it would be necessary to evaluate a potentially infinite series of truth functions in order to assign truth-values to propositions and evaluate the degree to which marketing claims and expressions are truthful. This would be impossible. In epistemology this is known as the regress problem (Audi 2011). Our solution to the problem is to assume that the internal brand universe or external reality provides sufficiently rich evidence to establish whether propositions are true or false. In cases where the analysis of this internal or external evidence under-determines whether a proposition is true or false, we assume that the proposition is false.[7] This procedure ensures that propositions will always have the binary value <true or false>: the minimum unit of analysis thereby provides a foundation from which truth analyses can progress.

The truth or falsity of propositions relies on a truth analysis along the dimensions of the correspondence, coherence and instrumental theories of truth. The result of this analysis depends on the personal judgement of the individual or groups of individuals who conduct the analysis and thereby contains an element of interpretation.[8] This, of course, allows room for failure. The consequence is that a given truth evaluation may be false. Propositions judged to be true may turn out to be false, and vice versa.

Truth-makers

A truth-maker expresses the conditions under which a given type of proposition is true. Philosophy is rich in discussions of the nature and role of truth-makers. MacBride (2014) observes that contemporary usage of the term 'truth-maker' is reflected in primitive form in, for example, Aristotle and Leibniz. There are multiple contemporary interpretations of what it means to be a truth-maker (MacBride 2014). Some accounts hold that the relation between a truth-bearer and its truth-maker is one of entailment, such that the content of the truth-maker logically entails the truth of the proposition. Others have argued that a truth-maker is some objective state of the world that necessitates that something is true. And there are many other accounts such as essentialism, axiomatism and truth as projection.

In this context, the notion of truth-maker is based upon Schaffer's (2008a, b, 2009, 2010) interpretation known as 'grounding'. Roughly, Schaffer holds that for any given context, C, a truth-maker is an entity that is grounded in C and makes one or more propositions, P, true in C because of its grounding properties, g, such that P is true in C to the extent that P(g). However, this definition under-determines the meaning of the fundamental feature of grounding. Schaffer proposes a contested solution (MacBride 2014), which we will not follow.

Let a truth-maker be a set of material or immaterial properties that are grounded in a relevant context and that make one or more propositions true. Properties are grounded in a given context to the extent that there is scientific or professional consensus on the importance of these characteristics in that context. We have defined truth of marketing expressions and claims as a multivalent function of the subclass relationship between functional, symbolic and behavioural propositions that are either true or false (binary truth). In this context, the relevant grounding properties are therefore the referents of functional, symbolic and behavioural claims. Let us have a closer look at these referents.

Functional claims state or imply that a product or service has certain properties and that use or consumption of the product satisfies a specific consumer need. The grounded truth properties are therefore product or service properties.[9]

Symbolic claims state or imply that using a specific product or service will associate the consumer with a certain identity or social group. The grounded truth properties should therefore be other consumers' perceptions of the brand and the symbolic or narrative identity of the brand universe. However, this intuitive solution is not viable because consumer perceptions and the identity of the brand universe are only partly the result of marketing efforts. Anker et al.'s (2015) paper on consumer dominant value creation demonstrates how consumers sometimes play a pivotal role in shaping – for better or worse – the image of a brand. Marketing is indeed a powerful tool to influence consumer perceptions, but it is not the only tool. As this exploration is exclusively concerned with the applied concept of truth embedded in marketing regulations – as opposed to the metaphysical concept of truth in marketing per se – I shall henceforth ignore consumer-created brand meanings. Accordingly, the scope of the grounded properties is restricted to the symbolic identity of the brand universe as established by means of a specified range of provider-driven marketing efforts.[10]

Behavioural claims state or imply that a product or service will allow a given state of affairs to obtain if the consumer adopts a specific course of action when using the product or service. The grounded properties are therefore the relevant patterns of consumption facilitated by the brand.[11]

Chapters 3–5 will flesh out how these grounded alethic properties make marketing claims true or false. Figure 1.1 summarizes the domain epistemology so far outlined.

1.5   Truth-values and truth measurement

The concept of truth-values plays multiple roles in philosophy, and there is significant disagreement on their ontological status and epistemic function (Shramko and Wansing 2015). Here, the function of truth-values is to establish the degree to which a marketing expression is true. The truth of

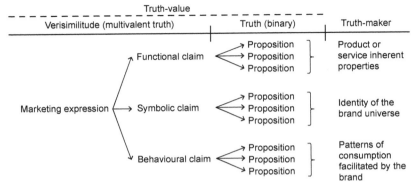

Figure 1.1 Alethic relationship between marketing expressions, claims and propositions.

expressions is conditional on the truth of subsets of claims and propositions. Each claim comprises a set of propositions that may be true or false. Any given set of propositions may therefore contain a mix of true and false propositions. The implication is that claims may have truth-content without being either true or false. This naturally transfers to expressions and explains why the theory of truth in marketing employs the multivalent concept of verisimilitude. The notion of truth-continuum operationalizes the function of verisimilitude or 'degree of truth'. See Figure 1.2.

The truth-continuum specifies degrees of truth on a scale from 0 to 100% such that any expression and claim will have a truth-value within this range. The total number of claims under scrutiny equals 100%. Each constituent proposition is assigned a binary truth-value: false propositions receive a truth-value of zero, whereas true propositions receive an average truth-value based on the total number of propositions included in the interrogation. Assume that a given truth analysis ranges over all three types of claims (functional, symbolic and behavioural) and each type of claim comprises a subset of three propositions. If true, each of the propositions represents 11.1%. The truth-values from each set of propositions is summed up and transferred to the relevant claim. Each claim now has a unique truth-value.

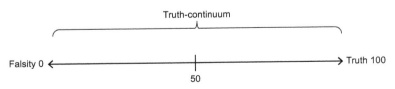

Figure 1.2 Truth-continuum.

The sum of these truth-values represents the truthfulness of the marketing expression per se, which is indicated on the truth-continuum as a truth-score.

An example will prove useful. Colgate is an internationally known dental care brand, producing products such as toothpaste, mouthwash and toothbrushes. The brand has a long history of advertising, stressing the functional and symbolic benefits of its product range. Recent ads make claims such as 'Active salt fights germs for healthy gums and teeth', 'Cavity protection', 'Sugar acid neutraliser', 'Contains fluoride' and 'Sensitivity protection'. These explicit claims are all functional. However, the visual narrative often stresses the symbolic benefits of having healthy, well cared for teeth: the brand strongly conveys the symbolic claim that healthy teeth – and thereby using their products – are instrumental to enjoying social peer recognition. Some ads – especially TV and YouTube videos – also feature experiential elements such as kids having fun when brushing their teeth. But the brand focus is heavily centred on functionality and the social status to which it is a tool. A truth analysis of Colgate can therefore relevantly exclude experiential claims.

For the sake of simplicity, make three assumptions. First, let there be a core functional and symbolic claim, each of which comprises three propositions. Second, assume that all functional propositions are thoroughly evidence based and thereby true. Finally, let the symbolic propositions be only partially justified. It is undoubtedly the case that fresh breath and clean white teeth are socially attractive, but the social popularity associated with some of the persons in various ads seems almost to indicate that dental health is a sufficient condition for social recognition and success. This is doubtful. Tables 1.1 and 1.2 provide an overview of the truth-content and

Table 1.1 Content breakdown of Colgate's functional and symbolic claims, propositions and overall brand expression.

	Colgate	
	Concept	
Construct	*Functional*	*Symbolic*
Expression	Colgate improves dental health and makes you socially attractive	
Claim	Colgate improves dental health	Colgate makes you socially attractive
Propositions	1 Contains fluoride 2 Strengthens tooth enamel 3 Protects against cavity and thereby provides the most important measure to address the most common cause of tooth decay	1 White teeth are associated with social success 2 Bad breath is socially unattractive 3 Using Colgate makes you popular

Table 1.2 Truth-score breakdown of Colgate's functional and symbolic propositions.

	Colgate			
	Proposition	*True*	*False*	*Truth-value*
Functional	Contains fluoride	+		16.7
	Strengthens tooth enamel	+		16.7
	Protects against cavity and thereby provides the most important measure to address the most common cause of tooth decay	+		16.7
Symbolic	White teeth are associated with social success	+		16.7
	Bad breath is socially unattractive	+		16.7
	Using Colgate makes you popular		–	0
	Truth-score		**83.5**	

truth-scores of Colgate's functional and symbolic claims. Figure 1.3 maps Colgate's truth-score onto the truth-continuum.

Weighted claims

Not all claims are equally important to a brand, and some claims may differ in importance relative to particular segments or international markets. Truth investigations may wish to take this into account such that there is a stronger epistemic weighting of core claims.

For Colgate, one can reasonably argue that functional claims enjoy primacy over symbolic claims, which in turn are more important to the brand than experiential claims. Another example could be Volvo, the carmaker, which has invested vast resources into research and development to enhance safety. Indeed, safety is very much the brand's point of difference in its traditional European markets. However, this classical brand position

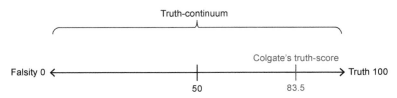

Figure 1.3 Colgate's unique truth-score.

is moderated in other markets such as the US and China, where the brand is positioned as sporty and executive. A truth analysis would therefore have to put different weight on the brand's functional and symbolic claims, weighting functional safety claims higher in Europe and symbolic claims higher in the US and China.

To avoid confusion, it is important to maintain a clear distinction between practical and epistemic importance. In practical terms, safety is *not* of less importance in the US and China; in epistemic terms it is. The truthfulness of a marketing expression is measured against a relevant section of the brand universe in a given market. Any type of claim may change in epistemic importance relative to market-specific brand differences and characteristics. The truth-content of a given claim, however, remains constant regardless of the epistemic weighting.

To demonstrate the practical impact of epistemic weighting, focus again on Colgate. Having examined Colgate's desired brand position, marketing campaigns and public perceptions, one can reasonably expect a truth investigation into the brand's marketing strategy to increase the epistemic weight of the functional claims. Accordingly, let functional claims amount to 70% of the brand position, and decrease the weight of the symbolic claims to 30%. Assuming that the truth-content is the same as in the previous example, the overall truth-score increases significantly (see Table 1.3).

Table 1.3 Weighted truth-scores for Colgate.

| | Colgate | | | | |
	Proposition	True	False	Truth-value	Weight
Functional	Contains fluoride	+		23.3	
	Strengthens tooth enamel	+		23.3	
	Protects against cavity and thereby provides the most important measure to address the most common cause of tooth decay	+		23.3	70%
Symbolic	White teeth are associated with social success	+		10	
	Bad breath is socially unattractive	+		10	30%
	Using Colgate makes you popular		−	0	
	Truth-score			**89.9**	

There is no unique formula or principle to determine the epistemic importance of a claim. The decision to assign epistemic primacy to a claim and the actual weighting of the claim rely on interpretation. The next section elaborates on the functional role of interpretation.

1.6 Interpretation, truth and objectivity

One may object that truth in marketing is a matter of interpretation and is thereby inevitably subjective. There is no doubt that establishing truth in marketing – and indeed in any other social discourse – requires a degree of interpretation. In this context, the only exception is functional claims that assert empirical propositions regarding product properties or features. Such propositions are testable with a minimum level of interpretation because the relevant truth-makers are physical facts. By contrast, the truth of symbolic and behavioural claims is contingent on relations to other epistemic entities (e.g., the wider brand narrative) and social facts and therefore implies a substantial level of interpretation. This, however, does not undermine key epistemic virtues such as professionalism, consistency and validity. Accordingly, interpretations are not necessarily subjective, as the following argument will demonstrate.[12]

Truth in marketing resembles the notion of truth in law. During the course of a legal trial, a series of different professionals such as the police, lawyers and judges make several decisions that are interpretive in nature (Dworkin 1982; Fiss 1982). To establish what is the case (Who did what to whom? How, why and when?), and how the law applies to the case, one has to understand the available evidence and its relation to the legal framework. These are interpretive acts. Some of the evidence may be hard facts (e.g., DNA from a blood sample on a weapon) that require a minimum level of interpretation. But a lot of evidence is narrative by nature such as documents, notes, letters, emails, and phone calls. Such evidence requires a much higher level of interpretation to establish what they truly are about. Although there is a substantial element of interpretation in a given epistemic practice such as law or social science, it is not justified to infer that these practices are subjective. Professional interpretation is guided by a range of principles (e.g., the principle of proportionality), epistemic virtues (e.g., coherence and validity) and institutional experience (e.g., precedence established by past adjudications and cases). In a similar way, the principle of what I call interpretive objectivity informs and directs truth interrogations in marketing.

The principle goes as follow: An interpretation, I, of the truthfulness of a marketing proposition, p, is non-subjective insofar as the interpreter(s) arrive at $I(p)$ as a result of an analysis, guided by professional experience, values and standards, of a relevant set of epistemic properties belonging to the set of brand entities (e.g., one ad, a set of ads, all marketing campaigns within a given period of time) under assessment. The relevant set of epistemic properties is specified by the grounding properties pertaining to functional, symbolic and behavioural claims and propositions.

Interpretation in action

Here are two examples of the role of interpretation in establishing truth in marketing. The first example involves a minimal level of interpretation, whereas the second involves a substantial degree of interpretation.

In May 2014, the Advertising Standards Authority UK[13] (ASA 2014a) ruled that a TV ad for Benecol yoghurt drinks was not allowed to be broadcast again. The ASA challenged whether the ad made unjustified health claims and stated as medical facts a number of unsubstantiated assertions. Our focus will be on the part of the adjudication that relates to the unsubstantiated assertion of medical facts. The TV ad stated:

> "Did you know two out of three adults have high cholesterol? Just like Linda here, until she discovered that ... certain foods lower cholesterol. Like Benecol which is proven to lower cholesterol by up to ten per cent in just three weeks". On-screen text stated "LOWER CHOLESTEROL UP TO 10% in 3 weeks". Smaller text stated "The plant stanols (1.5g–2.4g daily) in Benecol spreads, yoghurts or yoghurt drinks lowers [sic] cholesterol by 7–10% within 2–3 weeks as part of a healthy diet and lifestyle". The voiceover continued "Benecol, proven to lower cholesterol". Text also stated "PROVEN TO LOWER CHOLESTEROL".

To evaluate whether the asserted facts (e.g., 'Two out of three adults have high cholesterol') were substantiated, the ASA consulted a series of scientific medical reports submitted as evidence by the owner of the yoghurt brand, Johnson & Johnson. After a detailed comparison of the asserted health facts against the selected medical evidence the ASA found that there was no evidence that two-thirds of the UK population had high levels of cholesterol. On this ground, the ASA ruled the ad to be misleading (untruthful) and exaggerating the health benefit of the product.

The establishment of truth in this adjudication involves a minimal level of interpretation because the judgement is driven by an evaluation of empirical scientific evidence. However, the ruling is a good example of why all truth interrogations will involve an important component of interpretation: to establish whether the asserted health facts were substantiated, the ASA had to make an interpretative judgement as to whether the asserted facts were intended to apply to generally healthy adults or adults with increased risk of developing cardiovascular diseases. They found that the target audience would most likely perceive of the ad as indicating that two-thirds of all adults in the UK had high levels of cholesterol. Thus, although the scientific data, which form the baseline of the adjudication, are objective, the judgement as to the scope of the data (all adults or adults at risk) is an interpretative choice.

The second example is an ASA (2012a) adjudication on the clothing brand American Apparel. Two members of the public complained to the ASA that an ad for American Apparel appeared to sexualize a child. The ASA described the ad as follows:

> A press ad for American Apparel appeared on the back cover of Vice Magazine and pictured a girl sitting on an office chair wearing a jumper, knickers and knee-length socks. She was posed with her legs up on the chair and her knickers were visible.

The evaluation of the complaint is heavily interpretative and driven by contextual knowledge of the symbology of sex in contemporary society. The ASA considered that, although the ad did not contain explicit nudity, it nevertheless conveyed a sexualized impression of the model. Although she was over the age of 18, the model appeared to be under 16. The unsmiling expression on the model's face, the ASA found, "would be interpreted as having sexual undertones and a voyeuristic quality". The ASA banned American Apparel from publicizing the ad in its current form and impressed upon the firm not to depict any sexualized model who could appear to be a child. In this case, the truth about the actual content of the ad was established via a narrative interpretation of the cultural and symbolic meaning conveyed by a visual statement.

1.7 Conclusion

This chapter outlines a number of fundamental epistemological assumptions, on which the development of the theory of truth in marketing will build. Having clarified that the main object of the theory is propositional content, I categorized marketing content into three main constructs: marketing expressions, claims and propositions. Expressions are the most abstract and general form of content, for example, the totality of meaningful content associated with a brand, product or service. Expressions are made up of claims and propositions. Claims come in three different forms: functional, symbolic and behavioural. Each type of claim comprises a set of propositions, which are the minimal units of analysis.

Truth was broadly defined in two different ways. On the one hand, propositions are binary truth-bearers that are either true or false. They are made true or false by virtue of their relationship to relevant truth-makers. I roughly defined truth-makers in terms of grounded properties within the domain of marketing and subsequently identified truth-makers/grounded properties for functional, symbolic and behavioural content. On the other hand, the truth of claims and expressions is a function of subclass relationships: if all propositions are true, then all claims and the overall expression are true. However, if the propositional sets contain a mix of true and false propositions, then the correlated claims and the expression will have a truth-value somewhere on the continuum between true and false. Truth in this sense is thereby closely associated with the concept of verisimilitude (truthlikeness) as originally developed by Popper. I subsequently operationalized truth-values in terms of truth-scores. By way of example, different types of marketing claims were broken down into their constituent propositions and each proposition received a binary truth-score. These binary truth-scores were then assigned to claims and expressions, enabling quantitative truth measurement of marketing communications. The introduction of weighted claims created the opportunity for truth investigations to emphasize one particular communicative dimension of a brand, product or service.

Finally, the chapter discussed the role of interpretation. The analysis of two different ASA rulings demonstrated interpretation to play an integral part in establishing the truthfulness of marketing communications, even in the case of functional claims directly linked to a body of scientific evidence. However, the interpretative nature of truth in marketing does not necessarily lead to subjectivism and arbitrary decision making because interpretations have to satisfy a range of epistemic constraints such as professional values and coherence with past experience.

Notes

1 The concept, function and value of truth remain one of the central problems in contemporary philosophy. Wright and Pedersen's (2010a) collected volume, *New Waves in Truth*, showcases the continued vibrancy of propositional theories of truth across a range of classical and recent approaches, spanning the three core theoretical positions of monism, pluralism and deflationism. The book also covers hot topical discussions such as the relationship between truth and autonomy, the value of truth and different kinds of truth.

2 Other theoretical sociologists, notably Foucault, have critiqued the concept of truth. According to Foucault (1972, 1980, 2002), truth is not primarily a metaphysical or epistemic concept, but an inherently political construct that functions as a systemic vehicle to gain, control and exercise power. Although there is less emphasis on consumption in Foucault, his work provides a platform from which a critique much similar to that of Baudrillard could be launched.

3 Two streams of extant research address truth in marketing but without explicitly discussing the foundations of propositional truth. First, the extent to which marketing science is founded on a constructivist or realist concept of truth has been subject to some debate, following Hunt's (1990) seminal paper "Truth in Marketing Theory and Research". Second, a set of papers discusses truthfulness as a moral requirement in marketing (e.g., Attas 1999; Jackson 1990). The core question is the extent to which marketers have a moral obligation not to lie and deceive. The latter stream tacitly builds on a propositional theory of truth in marketing and is thereby closely associated with this project.

4 There may be marketing claims that fall outside the categories of functional, symbolic and behavioural claims. However, most marketing claims are analysable in terms of one of these three categories.

5 Section 1.5 discusses the notion of truth-continuum at greater length in connection with the practical application of the theory of truth in marketing.

6 Another important difference is that Popper applies the concept of verisimilitude to general theories that range across all domains of scientific enquiry, whereas verisimilitude in this exploration is context-specific. See Northcott (2013) for a detailed exposition of a context-specific model of verisimilitude.

7 Readers familiar with philosophical epistemology will be sensitive to the joint role assigned here to internal and external evidence. Mainstream epistemology assumes that truth is *either* an internal relation between epistemic entities (e.g., beliefs) *or* an external relation between statements and physical reality – never both. The reference to internal and external evidence as part of the same body of truth-making evidence is the first indication of this theory's pluralistic nature. The final chapter is devoted to the topic of alethic pluralism.

8 Section 1.6 and the last subsection of 6.2 elaborate on the function of interpretation in truth investigations.

9 Chapter 3 on the correspondence criterion of truth introduces the distinction between *inherent* and *supervenient* product/service properties. For the sake of clarity, I shall here ignore this distinction and simply talk of product/service properties as one uniform category.

10 Here, and consequently in Chapter 4, I exclude the alethic relevance of not just consumer-created brand perceptions, but also consumer perceptions established via marketing efforts. The reason is purely pragmatic: identifying consumer perceptions would require extensive consumer research, which would make truth investigations very laborious and time consuming. It would be empirically doable but practically uneconomic. Symbolic claims are therefore taken to be true or false relative to the symbolic values of the brand universe as intentionally created by marketers.

11 Chapter 5 distinguishes between direct and indirect facilitation of patterns of consumption. Direct facilitation requires interaction between the brand and the consumer during the consumption of the product, whereas indirect facilitation only requires that the brand suggests and encourages certain patterns of consumption for the consumer to pursue independently.

12 Chapter 6, Section 6.2, provides a related discussion of the problem of objectivity/subjectivity/relativity, but the focus is different: the key question is how to ensure objectivity within an epistemic framework (i.e., alethic pluralism) that triangulates three different theories of truth (correspondence, coherence and instrumentalism). The two discussions are conceptually distinct: the problem of interpretation would apply to all theories of truth in marketing regardless of whether they are monistic or pluralistic. By contrast, the problem of relativity would only apply to pluralism and some forms of monism (e.g., coherentism), but would not apply to others (e.g., the classical correspondence theory of truth).

13 The ASA's website (*https://www.asa.org.uk*) contains a searchable repository of all complaints and adjudications for the past five years. The database is a priceless resource to explore how advertising authorities and watchdogs understand, apply and – to some extent – construct truth in marketing. Especially in Chapters 3 and 4, I draw on ASA rulings to exemplify how the correspondence and coherence criteria apply to actual cases.

2   The classical pragmatic theory of truth

> 'The true,' to put it very briefly, is only the expedient in the way of our thinking, just as 'the right' is only the expedient in the way of our behaving. Expedient in almost any fashion; and expedient in the long run and on the whole of course ...
>
> William James, *Pragmatism*

2.1   The legacy of American pragmatism

Is truth one or many? Should a theory of truth in marketing adopt one universal definition of truth that ranges over the entire marketing domain and explains all accounts of truthfulness? Or do we need a pluralistic theory that integrates different ideas of truth to accommodate the complexity of marketing claims?

This book advocates a pluralistic approach and demonstrates how three different theories of truth explain the truth properties of three overarching categories of marketing claims. The theory builds on the legacy of American pragmatism. Although pragmatism is best known for the instrumental theory of truth, which links truthfulness with utility, key exponents such as William James (1842–1910) and Charles Sanders Peirce (1839–1914) are in fact alethic pluralists. They combine various ideas of truth into one framework in order to explain the multifaceted notion of scientific truth. The approach of this book is particularly indebted to Peirce and James's triangulation of the correspondence, coherence and instrumental theories of truth. This chapter introduces the classical pragmatic theory of truth and thereby establishes the platform from which the theory of truth in marketing progresses.

The American pragmatists have made two key contributions to the philosophical exploration of truth. Their first contribution is to demonstrate that the classical, competing theories of truth – correspondence and coherence – are integral components of one unified account of truth. The core insight is that correspondence and coherence theories capture important aspects of truth but cannot work as stand-alone accounts because truth is a multifaceted property that can be realized in many different ways. The second contribution is to introduce scientific consensus (to be reached at the end of inquiry) and utility or instrumentality as key indicators of propositional truth.

Thus, the overall contribution of the American pragmatists is to develop a unified framework that synthesizes four dimensions of truth: instrumentality, consensus, correspondence and coherence. See Forster (1996) and Haack (1976) for in-depth discussions of the differing roles of the four criteria in the works of Peirce, James and John Dewey (1859–1952). Below I have formulated the pragmatists' view of truth as a combination of all four criteria. The remainder of this chapter unpacks the meaning of the definition.

Pragmatic definition of truth
A propositional claim that P is true insofar as: (a) holding and acting on P is useful to the agent, A, over time; (b) P corresponds to some external state of affairs and this referential relation coheres with A's actual and future experience; (c) P would be believed or agreed by all rational agents at the end of a sustained process of scientific inquiry.

The pragmatists' holistic view of truth developed into various forms of alethic pluralism, often motivated by the observation that truth properties seem to fluctuate across domains (Pedersen and Wright 2013). Contemporary alethic pluralists address truth as a concept possessing core properties that are realizable in multiple ways, depending on the context of inquiry (Lynch 2004, 2009; Wright 1992, 1993, 1998) or communicative discourse (Apel 1980, 1982). In Chapter 6, the discussion of the meta-justification of the theory of truth in marketing will return to the contemporary debate on alethic pluralism.

The theory of truth in marketing resonates strongly with the main thrust of the classical pragmatic view of truth. First, the fundamental assumption of the theory is that the domain of marketing comprises at least three different types of claims, each of which calls for a different type of truth evaluation and thereby involves a pragmatic triangulation of different theories of truth. The pragmatic insistence on truth as a multiple realizable property and the willingness to mix opposing theories of truth to grasp the multifaceted, complex nature of truth inform the entire development of the theory of truth in marketing. Second, the genuine pragmatic idea of linking truth to practice, experience and, especially, utility and instrumentality (Misak 2013) has enabled the development of a marketing-specific instrumental criterion of truth that can accommodate and test the veracity of behavioural marketing claims.

But the theory of truth in marketing also differs substantially from classical pragmatism. First, the theories of Peirce, James and Dewey build on distinct ontologies and epistemologies, and buying into these would not be conducive to the development of a marketing-specific theory of truth. For example, Peirce's theory of truth rests on his theory of signs, and using his pragmatic framework would thereby entail a commitment to a certain epistemology, which again would have ontological implications and require a certain stance on realism or idealism.

Second, the classical pragmatic formulations of truth cannot be applied directly to marketing because of the differing domains of exploration. Pragmatism operates in scientific contexts where the epistemic agent is a scientist testing empirical hypotheses (Misak 2013). The focal point is the epistemic relationship between one class of epistemic agents and the external non-human world. The unit of analysis is observations. By contrast, this exploration operates in a social domain, with a number of epistemic agents spanning various stakeholders such as consumers, customers, marketers, adjudicators and policymakers. The focal points are both the epistemic relationship between the different classes of epistemic agents and the external non-human world *and* the inter-relationship between the different classes of epistemic agents. The units of analysis are communications (conveyed by verbal and symbolic narratives and embedded in behaviours) as they unfold and are interpreted in social contexts and their references to the external non-human world.

Third, the pragmatic consensus criterion – that is, the view that truth ultimately reflects consensus among rational epistemic agents at the end of scientific inquiry – is not part of the core theory of truth in marketing. Though relevant and applicable in the marketing domain, the consensus criterion is primarily of importance to the understanding of how policymakers agree on marketing standards and regulation, which define – though incompletely – what truthfulness in marketing is. The consensus criterion is redundant to the alethic scrutiny of functional, symbolic and behavioural marketing claims.

Finally, the correspondence and coherence theories of truth have been subject to considerable development and are still central to the contemporary debate on truth. Benefitting from these more recent developments would be constrained by the adoption of any given pragmatic theory of truth and the implicit import of a distinct ontology and epistemology.

2.2   The pragmatic maxim

The pragmatic maxim is often taken to encapsulate the essence of classical pragmatic philosophy (Hookway 2012, 2015). The maxim is not just of interest to the contemporary exploration of the modern history of philosophy (Misak 2013) but continues to inform developments of the very notion of pragmatic truth (Howat 2014; Legg 2014; Stango 2015). The maxim comes in various formulations, the most famous being the following one by Peirce (1986, 266) in his *How to Make Our Ideas Clear*:

> … consider what effects, which might conceivably have practical bearings, we conceive the object of our conception to have. Then, our conception of those effects is the whole of our conception of the object.

Put differently, the maxim holds that the meaning of a concept is defined in terms of the consequences believing in or applying that concept makes in a practical context. This interpretation is in line with Olshewsky's (1983) observation that the pragmatic maxim should be understood in terms of Peirce's (1986, 265) remark that "the whole function of thought is to produce habits of action". Two dimensions are crucial to the understanding of the maxim: the link between practical consequences and truth; and the meaning of the concept of practical consequences.

Standard interpretations take the maxim to implicitly make the controversial claim that meaning and truth are semantically linked to practical consequences (Hookway 2012; Misak 2013): meaning and truth are concerned with human experience, practice and the outcome of our actions. An abundance of remarks and discussions in both Peirce and James support this interpretation, as seen, for example, in this quote from James's (1975a, 51) *The Meaning of Truth*: "thoughts are true which guide us to *beneficial interaction* with sensible particulars."

As such, the maxim conveys the essence of the general pragmatic idea of truth, which is provided above. Firmly grounded in the maxim is especially the definition's first condition that in order to understand the veracity of a propositional entity (e.g., a claim or belief) we need to establish the practical consequences of holding and acting on that entity (i.e., usefulness over time).

Although Peirce and James agree on the controversial linkage between truth and practical consequences, they provide differing accounts of the type of consequences that fall within the scope of the pragmatic theory of truth. Peirce's notion of truth-relevant practical consequences is linked to his view on the convergence of scientific knowledge (Hookway 2000). In *How to Make Our Ideas Clear*, Peirce argues that the scientific method – that is, the empirical natural sciences – ultimately arrives at a shared understanding of a given scientific topic at the end of inquiry. He states (1986, 273): "The opinion which is fated to be ultimately agreed to by all who investigate, is what we mean by truth."

Peirce thus advocates a blend of epistemic collectivism and falsificationism: truth is determined as agreement or consensus among members of epistemically privileged scientific communities. Truth-relevant practical consequences are thereby the results of scientific tests, and, consequently, the justification or falsification of theories and hypotheses. The related instrumental criterion of truth should thereby be understood in terms of whether a given type of behaviour (i.e., a given application of the scientific method) is useful to the scientific community and collective exploration of the empirical world.

In contrast to Peirce's epistemic collectivism, James offers an individualistic account of truth-relevant practical consequences. Roughly, the account can be formulated as follows: If A were to believe that P, and if A's believing that P would motivate A to adopt a certain course of action that would create beneficial consequences for A, then P would be true. This is a form of epistemic existentialism where alethic properties are relative to their practical impact on the life world of individual epistemic agents. Moore (1907) and Russell (1992) dismissed this idea because acting on a false belief may produce positive consequences and acting on true beliefs may be utterly useless. For example, believing in God may prove existentially useful to many people even if God does not exist.

The devil is in the detail, though, and this criticism does not fully take into account the pragmatic emphasis on successful agency *over time*. As Haack (1976, 238) argues, the pragmatic link between truth and practical consequences or utility should be construed in terms of true beliefs being "guaranteed against overthrow by subsequent experience". This means that acting on a false belief can be useful in the short term only: relying on false beliefs to guide one's actions across numerous time-sections is likely to be counterproductive, given the increased risk of the false belief becoming destabilized by losing its fit with practical experience.[1]

The reason why the pragmatic maxim is seen as capturing the essence of pragmatic philosophy is now clear: the maxim motivates the introduction of both the instrumental and the consensus criteria of truth. The maxim's implicit insistence on meaning and truth as determined by practical consequences creates the pivotal link to understanding truth instrumentally as utility in scientific (Peirce) or everyday (James) contexts. Peirce's conceptualization of truth-relevant practical consequences as convergence of opinion among scientists provides the link to the consensus criterion. Figure 2.1 summarizes the discussion of the pragmatic maxim.

2.3   Preliminary remarks on the pragmatic theory of truth

Traditionally, philosophers adhere strictly to the principle of parsimony and therefore argue in favour of one specific theory of truth. This is a tendency that is motivated by defensive concerns, predominantly the perceived need to develop theories that resist all types of counterexamples. The American pragmatists are less concerned with developing flawless theories and are fundamentally motivated by increasing the explanatory power of scientific theories.

The driving intuition is that the complexity of the world exceeds the explanatory power of existing, mono-theoretical accounts of truth because truth manifests itself in many different ways. Theories should represent a scientific, empirically testable view of the world: if the world happens to be fundamentally complex and multidimensional, then we have to accept the need for complex theories that merge different conceptual frameworks. The price to be paid in terms of increased vulnerability to criticism and

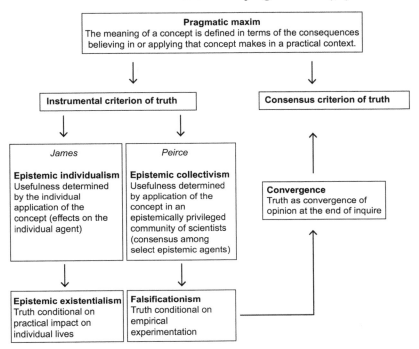

Figure 2.1 Overview of the conceptual relations between the pragmatic maxim and the instrumental and consensus criteria of truth.

counterexamples is nothing compared to the significant gain in explanatory power. This explains why Peirce, James and Dewey attempt to develop a grand theory that unifies various accounts of truth. The following sections briefly introduce the four criteria of truth employed in classical pragmatic philosophy.

Whether the key exponents of American pragmatism should be interpreted as working on the same grand theory of truth or as individual philosophers with distinct contributions within a roughly delineated field is subject to debate. Haack (1976) and Forster (1996) have convincingly argued that despite the important differences between the pragmatists, they are working on the same fundamental project. They all aim at developing a pluralistic theory of truth grounded in instrumental and consensus criteria of truth. Peirce provides the seminal contribution, and James and Dewey significantly develop and refine the original theory into a set of interlocking claims, assumptions and hypotheses.

One important difference between Peirce and James is their stance on nominalism. I highlight this difference here because it has bearing on truth in marketing. The debate over nominalism concerns the ontological status of universals and abstract objects. Nominalists reject the existence of universals such as 'redness' and only accept the existence of particular things that are red, that is, a red car. The same applies to abstract objects, which do not exist in space or time, but as ideas, concepts or types. Abstract objects are, for example, 'language' as opposed to a specific language such as English; 'tennis' as opposed to a specific game of tennis; or 'car' as opposed to a specific car on the road. Peirce operates with universals and abstract objects as real entities, whereas James denies their existence. The theory of truth in marketing will follow Peirce on this point: brands are clear examples of abstract objects, and any theory of truth in marketing will therefore have to be committed to a non-nominalist metaphysics.

Doubt and the search for truth

According to the pragmatists, humans are not preoccupied with truth because the concept is of interest per se. The reason we care about the abstract phenomenon of truth is that it has practical ramifications for the everyday business of life. In Peirce's theory of truth, doubt – and its impact on human agency – is the main epistemic driver that initiates explorations of the concept of truth. He puts it this way (Peirce 1986, 247–248):

> The irritation of doubt causes a struggle to attain a state of belief. I shall term this struggle *inquiry.* ... The irritation of doubt is the only immediate motive for the struggle to attain belief. ... With the doubt, therefore, the struggle begins, and with the cessation of doubt it ends. Hence, the sole object of inquiry is the settlement of opinion.

Peirce shares the emphasis on doubt as the root of epistemology with the philosophical tradition that began with Descartes' (2013) meditations and developed into that predominant stream of modern analytic epistemology, which is largely motivated by finding a convincing reply to what is known as global (Klein 2000) or radical (Audi 2011) skepticism.

However, the pragmatic and Cartesian notions of doubt are not to be conflated. In Descartes' epistemology the entire belief system comes into doubt because he realizes that all our beliefs are fallible (i.e., global skepticism). Peirce agrees that all our beliefs are fallible, but he rejects the idea of global skepticism. The totality of our belief system and our entire epistemic outlook is not subject to doubt and, crucially, cannot be because doubt is only possible against a background of certainty (local skepticism). To doubt is for an agent, A, to be in a situation where some state of affairs, x causes A to doubt a belief that P, because P suddenly seems unstable when A interprets x in light of the totality of her experience and other beliefs. In order for A to doubt that P, she needs to have a large set of stable beliefs that unsettles P by calling it into doubt. Figure 2.2 demonstrates Peirce's notion of doubt.

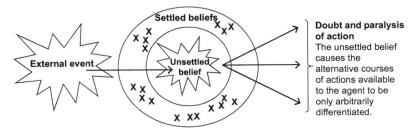

Figure 2.2 Pierce's idea of doubt as unsettled belief.

Doubt is the driver of the exploration of the concept of truth because it causes paralysis of action (Misak 2013). The underlying assumption that makes sense of this idea is the intricate link between belief and agency. Peirce often conceptualizes beliefs as habits of action. In *The Fixation of Belief* (Peirce 1986, vol. 3, p. 247), he describes the relation between belief and agency as follows: "Belief does not make us act at once, but puts us into such a condition that we shall behave in a certain way, when the occasion arises."

Beliefs dispose an agent to adopt certain courses of actions. *True* beliefs enable the agent to engage *successfully* in a range of different courses of actions.[2] When a belief is called into doubt, unsettled by external events, then the agent is no longer able to act efficiently because the pattern of action, which the belief used to enable, is no longer available as a convincing choice. When one is in a state of doubt, two or more courses of action seem equally relevant, promising or right, which causes an inability to act rationally. Action is, of course, possible but only as an arbitrary inclination.

Accordingly, the aim of epistemology is to clarify the rules of justified fixation of belief, whereas the aim of science (i.e., the natural sciences) is to execute the process of stabilizing unsettled beliefs and corroborate new beliefs via empirical discovery and experimentation.

False methods of fixation of belief

Before I outline the pragmatic process of belief-stabilization and fixation, it will be useful to briefly discuss what Peirce sees as the main flawed ways of belief-fixation.

First, some people have a tendency to hold on to their beliefs and assumptions regardless of what conflicting evidence the world may throw at them. Peirce (1986, vol. 3, 250–254) terms this *tenacity*. Prejudice against other people, for example, is often an epistemic coping mechanism to safeguard a belief-set from exposure to potentially conflicting evidence. But negating the relevance of the viewpoint of one group of people (say, the UK Government downplaying Scotland's desire for independence) or a specific type of theory (such as creationists negating the ideas of biological evolution) is a flawed way of belief-fixation because the associated beliefs (in constitutional unity or God) would be overthrown if the agents holding the beliefs were willing to accept empirical evidence from the social and natural sciences. Tenacity resolves the paralysis of action caused by doubt, but the resultant belief-stabilization is fragile as empirical evidence constantly challenges the underpinning beliefs. Moreover, tenacity is not just epistemically fragile; it is also practically unsatisfactory because the inherent prejudice by default rules out a number of courses of actions which could be very productive or useful. In this sense, tenacity runs counter to the pragmatic truth criterion of utility, which will be discussed below.

Second, this negative form of epistemic tenacity is often carried out by totalitarian states rather than by individuals. Peirce (1986, vol. 3, 251) dubs this second way of unwarranted belief fixation 'the method of authority'. Authoritarianism has certain advantages compared to individual tenacity. Historic evidence suggests that indoctrinating certain principles and values into the mind-set of whole populations may be productive in some respects. Peirce mentions that many of the world's greatest examples of architecture such as the Egyptian pyramids are the product of the method of authority. However, over time authoritarianism will inevitably be undermined by the societal outliers (such as true scientists) that do not respect the doctrines and only accept values and principles that are formed as a result of empirical observation of the social and natural world. Authoritarianism is thus vulnerable to formation of doubt that will lead to unresolvable paralysis of action because the doctrines do not allow the open-minded scientific discovery and experimentation needed to find solutions and define new directions of travel for the society.

Finally, and from a philosophical point of view most importantly, Peirce (1986, vol. 3, 253–255) rejects the a priori method as a route to belief-fixation (Skagestad 1981). Here the pragmatists again clash directly with Cartesian philosophy and much of the modern analytic tradition of epistemology (Audi 2011; Dancy 1998). Descartes solves the problem of doubt by pointing to one – the one and only – belief that one cannot doubt: the *cogito*, the fact that if I doubt, I must exist. From this a priori truth, Descartes rebuilds his belief system. The pragmatic tradition rejects the a priori method and insists that all true or warranted beliefs must come from our experience of the external world. The only justified way of belief-fixation is through empirical observation. The pragmatists are thereby frontrunners of naturalized epistemology as later developed by Quine (Kornblith 1994; Quine 2002).

The underlying diagnosis of the problem and the inadequacy of the a priori method should be found in the account of doubt given above and the distinction between global and local skepticism. According to the a priori method, everything is in principle subject to doubt: Descartes formulates the seminal argument that because all indicators and criteria of certainty could appear in a dream, then there is nothing that logically prevents the conclusion that we may be fictitious products of a dream. However, the fact that I doubt means that I exist, and this observation then becomes the bedrock upon which all other beliefs will rest. To the pragmatists, this a priori way of building an epistemology is fundamentally flawed because the very starting point – the concept of doubt – is erroneous. As described, the pragmatic epistemology holds that doubt can only appear against a backdrop of settled beliefs because a belief becomes doubtful when an agent reflects on new empirical evidence in light of her actual experience. Pragmatic truth is thereby radically empiricist in nature. The following quote demonstrates Peirce's (1986, 253) view on the matter:

> To satisfy our doubts, therefore, it is necessary that a method should be found by which our beliefs may be caused by nothing human, but by some external permanency – by something upon which our thinking has no effect.

2.4   The pragmatic theory of truth

The preceding sections have established that (a) the problem of truth begins with one of our beliefs being called into question and becoming unsettled in light of new external evidence; (b) this uncertainty results in a paralysis of action; and (c) scientific inquiry is the ultimate means by which the unsettled belief can be replaced or justified, discarded or settled. Science is thereby a process of fixation of belief and, in turn, a way of restoring the normal practical order, where humans can act successfully based on rational assessment of the external state of affairs against the totality of their belief-set. The question that needs answering now is how the process of belief-fixation (justification of belief) unfolds. How do we test claims, beliefs and propositions for truthfulness on the pragmatic account of truth?

As mentioned, the pragmatic theory of truth answers the question by unifying four distinct truth criteria – correspondence, coherence, consensus and instrumentalism – into a unified theory of truth. I will now unpack the meaning of each criterion and provide an interpretation of their inter-relations. The criteria are very much interlocking aspects of truth. My attempt to address them separately is solely for the purpose of analytic clarity.

Correspondence

The first element of belief-fixation that leads towards establishing the truth or falsity of a propositional entity P (e.g., a belief, claim or statement) is to establish the relation of P to external reality. In its most generic form, the correspondence theory holds that P is true insofar as P *corresponds* to some external fact. Thus, the claim 'The cat is on the mat' is true to the extent that there actually is a cat on the mat. Some of the main issues associated with the correspondence theory are to provide a satisfactory account of what is meant by 'external facts' and what it is for a propositional entity 'to correspond' to such external facts. Before addressing the pragmatists' view on these issues, it will prove useful to first establish their commitment to some variant of the correspondence theory.

The pragmatists' stance on the correspondence condition of truth is contested. Misak (2013), for example, interprets Peirce and James as strong opponents of the theory, whereas Haack (1976) and Forster (1996) argue that the pragmatic theory of truth contains strong correspondence elements, although they provide differing accounts of the nature of the correspondence relation. The following quotes demonstrate James and Peirce's commitment to some variant of the correspondence theory of truth. In the opening of his lecture *Pragmatism's Conception of Truth*, James (1975b, 96) states that:

> Truth, as any dictionary will tell you, is a property of certain of our ideas. It means their 'agreement,' as falsity means their disagreement, with 'reality'. Pragmatists and intellectualists both accept this definition as a matter of course. They begin to quarrel only after the question is raised as to what may precisely be meant by the term 'agreement,' and what by the term 'reality,' when reality is taken as something for our ideas to agree with.

Peirce (1986, 282) puts the same idea this way:

> Truth consists in the existence of a real fact corresponding to the true proposition ... a true proposition corresponds to *a real matter of fact*, by which is meant a state of things, definite and individual, which *does not consist merely in being represented (in any particular representation) to be as it is.*

What do the pragmatists' mean by 'reality/external fact' and 'correspondence'? The discussion of reality takes place at both a metaphysical and practical level. Metaphysically, the key issue is whether pragmatic epistemology necessarily buys into a realist or anti-realist ontology.[3] Forster (1996) suggests a realist interpretation and argues that Peirce thought of correspondence as a relation between a propositional entity, P, and external objects that exist independently from how we think they are. Reality is *not* constituted by our constructs of meaning; rather, the meaning of a proposition is fixed through its reference to an external object that exists in and of itself.

This realist interpretation of Peirce runs counter to various of his observations on the relation between thought and reality. The following quote clearly demonstrates that Peirce (1986, 56), at least to some extent, conceptualizes correspondence as an anti-realistic condition.

> [S]ome metaphysicians say that a true conception is one which *corresponds to* a thing existing independent of all thought. But nothing is gained by substituting one relation of reason for another; a thing corresponds to another only so far as the mind regards them as correlates. It would be quite beside the purpose to say that a true conception is one which is *produced by* something existing out of thought. ... Every way considered therefore there is a complete vacuity of meaning in saying that independent of all thought there exist such things as we shall think in the final opinion.

Inspired by the first quote, Haack (1976, 243) offers an anti-realistic understanding of the correspondence relation and argues that in pragmatic epistemology "correspondence with reality *is* coherence with the totality of experience". The problem with this interpretation is that it is difficult to understand what the correspondence criterion contributes, which is not already entailed by the coherence criterion. By reducing correspondence to coherence with experience, the concept becomes superfluous.

My suggestion is to understand correspondence as a *practico-epistemic* rather than *metaphysical* concept. This idea builds on Peirce's definition of belief as habit of action and operates in the intersections between realism and anti-realism. Insofar as beliefs are habits of action, they are correlated with the external consequences of these actions. Correspondence then means the establishment of a referential relation between A's belief that P and the consequences of the pattern of action encouraged by believing that P. Correspondence thereby becomes a tracking condition between external states of affairs (consequences correlated with the belief that P) and the actual belief that P. This interpretation cuts across the realism/anti-realism distinction: the relevant external facts (consequences of action) exist independently of the mind, but they are still causally correlated to the mind because they are the result of the behavioural disposition entailed in believing that P. This interpretation makes sense of pragmatism's under-determined stance on realism versus anti-realism and also fits excellently with the genuinely pragmatic idea of instrumental truth, which will be discussed below.

Against this background, I suggest the following definition of the pragmatic account of truth as correspondence. Let an agent, A, believe that P in a given context, C. Then, P corresponds in a truth-conducive way to some external reality, X, insofar as X is a successful consequence of the habit or pattern of action enabled by holding and acting on P. In other words, for any belief that P, the truth-conducive correspondence characteristic is the referential relation between P and the successful consequences of holding and acting on P.

This definition raises the question of epistemic success: under what circumstances does holding and acting on a belief initiate a successful pattern of action? The short answer is that successful agency coheres with experience. This provides a conceptual link to the coherence criterion, which is the focus of the next subsection.

Coherence

The coherence and correspondence theories agree that truth is a relational property. But the theories disagree over what type of properties function as truth conditions, and they give differing accounts of the nature of alethic relations.

As we saw, the correspondence theory holds that truth conditions are external states of affairs. By contrast, coherentists turn away from external reality and embed all alethic features internally in the cognitive outlook of the agent. The ultimate test of truth and justification is the extent to which a proposition bears the right relation to other propositions. Propositions are thereby the truth conditions of other propositions. In terms of alethic relations, the theories obviously disagree over whether it is correspondence or coherence that is truth-conducive. In essence, standard coherence theories of truth hold that a proposition is true insofar as it coheres with other propositions in a specified set of propositions (Young 2001).

Both Peirce and James rely on some elements of the coherence theory of truth. And in both writers, the coherence theory seems to be intertwined with the correspondence theory such that the two theories appear as complementary rather than competing accounts of truth. The following quote from Peirce (1986, 34) demonstrates the intimate connection between the coherence and correspondence criteria of truth.

> [I]f we mount the stream of thought instead of descending it, we see each thought caused by previous thought, until at last we reach the original sensations, which it is supposed themselves are caused by something external. In using the word "supposed," I do not wish to imply that there is any room for doubt in the matter; but only that the external realities are not themselves the immediate object of thought but are only what it is necessary to suppose exist, to account for the phenomena of sensation. We find in this stream of thought, in this succession of images, a certain coherency, harmony or consistency, which can not be due entirely to the laws of association themselves; but which extends into the additions which are made to the body of our thought from without. And it is this coherency of experience which demonstrates the existence of reality; or something permanent and fixed, to which our thought and experience, more or less perfectly, corresponds.

Here, coherence is a condition of justification in terms of consistency of thought and experience, but the quote also shows how coherence is a metaphysical principle: reality is constituted by coherent experience. Moreover, our thoughts and experience correspond to the reality constituted by the coherence of experience. The pragmatic application of the coherence theory departs significantly from the standard account. Where the core feature of the standard account is that propositions are justified through their relations to other propositions, the pragmatic interpretation introduces a coherence relation between individual experience and reality.

This is controversial, but a logical consequence of Peirce's definition of beliefs as grounding patterns of action. The argument goes as follows: (a) a belief is a habit of action that grounds a certain behavioural pattern; (b) beliefs are thereby naturally correlated with external correlates in the form of the practical consequences of the belief-entailed actions; (c) this means that the coherence of a belief-set is naturally dependent on external correlates (i.e., practical consequences). This reading of the pragmatists' understanding of coherence suggests the following definition: A's belief that P is true insofar as the consequences of the pattern of action that holding P entails cohere with the totality of A's experience.

Though provocative, the pragmatic understanding of coherence offers a solution to one of the most fundamental problems – the plurality objection[4] – associated with standard coherence theories of truth. The expression of truth exclusively in terms of relations between propositions creates a disconnect between truth and external reality. The implication is a loss of any independent measure of truth: two persons may have radically different and mutually incompatible belief-sets, which – analyzed in isolation – are perfectly coherent. The coherence theory does not guarantee or presuppose any kind of cross-domain or inter-subjective convergence. Thus, coherentists are faced with a two-fold problem. On the one hand, they have to accept the incoherent conclusion that two incompatible accounts of the same phenomenon can both be equally true. On the other, they also have to accept the incoherent conclusion that a coherent theory that runs counter to obvious empirical evidence must still be accepted as true. The pragmatic interpretation of the coherence criterion of truth provides the connection to external reality that is necessary to avoid the objections: beliefs understood as grounding habits of action are by definition associated with an external correlate (practical consequences) that works as the measurement of coherence.

Consensus

In its most general form, the consensus theory of truth states that truth is determined by epistemic standards and principles of discovery agreed within a community of epistemic agents. Truth, to use Dewey's terminology, becomes a form of warranted assertability. The test of whether a propositional claim or belief is true is therefore to be found in contextual rules of validity and justification as constituted within a given context of discovery. Consensus theories have a strong element of inter-subjectivism, which easily leads to relativism about truth. I will now provide a rough sketch of the pragmatists' idea of consensus and discuss how they avoid the problem of relativism.

Peirce's motivation for adopting a consensus criterion of truth is grounded in his critique of the correspondence theory of truth. He holds that it is impossible to check and evaluate the relation between our propositions and reality from a neutral standpoint outside our situated relation to reality. Consensus between privileged epistemic agents (i.e., the scientific community) is therefore a necessary component of any attempt to settle the veracity of a propositional claim or scientific theory.

Peirce's (1986, 25) commitment to some variant of the consensus theory of truth is supported by the following quotes.

> Unless we make ourselves hermits, we shall necessarily influence each other's opinions; so that the problem becomes how to fix belief, not in the individual merely, but in the community.

> In sciences in which men come to agreement, when a theory has been broached it is considered to be on probation until this agreement is reached. After it is reached, the question of certainty becomes and idle one, because there is no one left who doubts it. We individually cannot reasonably hope to attain the ultimate philosophy which we pursue; we can only seek it, therefore, for the *community* of philosophers.

The emphasis on agreement and settlement of belief and opinion is a clear indication of a consensus element: the true nature of the external reality cannot be described without recourse to epistemic standards determined through agreement in a community of privileged epistemic agents. Science is not just an empirical enterprise of testing and evaluation of theories and hypotheses; it is also effectively a social endeavour driven by (a) the need to reach agreement and (b) the fact that humans are social beings.

The need for agreement is closely linked to Peirce's characteristic of science as driven by doubt and aiming at settling beliefs that has been put in doubt. As discussed, doubt causes paralysis of action, and all activities that are presupposed on a belief, which has been called into doubt, therefore come to a halt. Doubt is an epistemic impasse that not only affects our intellectual understanding of the world but – given the pragmatic understanding of belief as habit of action – causes a breakdown of societal practice, science included. We need to reach epistemic agreement in order to carry out our various different activities.

This observation does not make science a social enterprise as such but merely makes the epistemic standards conditional on social agreement in scientific communities. However, the second quote clearly connects Peirce with a social-epistemological conceptualization of the search for scientific truth. Scientists necessarily influence each other's opinions, and the overarching problem of truth and knowledge becomes a question of social epistemology: how do we settle beliefs in social discourse?

It is tempting to dismiss the consensus aspects of the pragmatic theory of truth with reference to the problem of cultural relativism: if truth is necessarily conditioned on social agreement in specified scientific communities, then it is perfectly possible for two different scientific communities to agree on different epistemic principles and, consequently, produce equally true, but mutually incompatible, theories.

One strength of alethic pluralism is that the triangulation of different theories or criteria of truth increases the explanatory power and reinforces the ability to address standard objections. In this case, the inclusion of the coherence and correspondence elements of truth provides an internal and external anchor point against which consensus should be reached. Consensus is *not* an arbitrary settlement of opinion. Consensus, as both Apel (1980, 1982) and Habermas (2003) argue, occurs as discursive settlement of ideas among rational, communicative agents who are constrained by our empirical observation of external facts and language's a priori structuring of our entire perception of the world. When immersed in rational discourse such as in a scientific community, it is *not* possible to attain agreement of arbitrary statements and hypotheses: rational agents will only agree to a given theory about the natural or social world if there is agreement that the theory is an epistemically satisfying representation or description of the domain of inquiry. And that agreement – given that the domain of inquiry is populated with rational agents – will only be reached if the theory under consideration will be seen as cohering with extant experience and corresponding to the shared perception of the world. This is why Peirce characterizes truth as the convergence of opinion and Dewey claims that truth is the end of inquiry: if the process if inquiry were to be carried out infinitely, then all rational agents would ultimately agree on the same opinion and assume the same overall belief-set.

Finally, the consensus criterion is a necessary component in the pragmatists' epistemic outlook: although the pragmatists do not accept Cartesian doubt where all our beliefs are put to doubt at the same time, they very much agree that all of our beliefs are, in principle, potentially false and therefore always potential candidates for radical doubt. In other words, global skepticism is dismissed because we cannot meaningfully dissociate ourselves from the totality of our belief system, but skepticism nevertheless has a global reach in the sense that no matter how deep rooted and fundamental a belief is, it is potentially false. Peirce puts it this way:

> I do not say that it is infallibly true that there is any belief to which a person would come if he were to carry his inquiries far enough. I only say that that alone is what I call truth. I cannot infallibly know that there *is* any truth.[5]

The quote clearly expresses a commitment to falsificationism, which is the view that any given scientific theory should be clearly connected to the observable world such that empirical investigation can demonstrate whether the theory is false, but that it is impossible to conclude whether it is true.[6] Here the implication is that regardless of how far scientific inquiry continues, it will never actually hit upon truth, although it will continuously converge towards it. As inquiry continues and the scientific community keeps falsifying a particular theory, it becomes increasingly likely that the theory is true, but – given the assumption that all beliefs and assumptions are potentially false – we will never be in a position to say with absolute certainty that a given theory or hypothesis is true.

What Peirce means by true is thereby the cluster of theories and belief-sets that rational agents decide to agree upon at the end of inquiry.[7] In this sense, truth is fundamentally influenced by empirical investigation, but it is ultimately determined by the conditions of warranted assertability in social communities of rational agents. The process of determining truth is a dialectic development where consensus is reached based on an inter-subjective interpretation of the extent to which observable facts cohere with collective experience and correspond to external reality.

Based on this discussion, I define the pragmatic consensus criterion of truth as follows: A's belief that P is true insofar as a community of rational agents agrees to assert P as true in light of a critical interpretation of the extent to which P coheres with actual, collective experience *and* corresponds to our conception of external reality established via continued empirical inquiry of P.

Instrumentalism

The notorious pragmatic slogan 'The truth is what works' epitomizes the core of the instrumental criterion of truth (Cormier 2001). As James (1975b, 44; 97) puts it:

> [Pragmatism's] only test of probable truth is what works best in the way of leading us, what fits every part of life best and combines with the collectivity of experience's demands, nothing being omitted.

> Pragmatism, on the other hand, asks its usual question. "Grant an idea or belief to be true," it says, "what concrete difference will its being true make in anyone's actual life? How will the truth be realized? What experiences will be different from those which would obtain if the belief were false? What, in short, is the truth's cash-value in experiential terms?"

As the quotes suggest, an instrumental theory of truth expresses truth in terms of practical functions. The general idea is that a propositional entity P (i.e., a belief, claim, statement) is true if A's holding and acting on P makes a positive contribution to the practical undertakings of A. Peirce and James agree on this core assumption, but their instrumental accounts of truth differ fundamentally owing to their disagreement over nominalism (i.e., the ontological status of universals and abstract entities). Before entering this discussion, it will prove beneficial to first establish a broader picture of the general pragmatic idea of truth as usefulness.

Peirce's definition of belief is the underlying assumption, which configures pragmatic epistemology to adopt an instrumental criterion of truth. "The essence of belief," Peirce (1986, 263–264) holds, "is the establishment of a habit, and different beliefs are distinguished by the different modes of action to which they give rise". Epistemology as such is intimately linked to practical agency because propositional attitudes (e.g., beliefs) – the core building block of the world-view of any rational agent – dispose us to adopt certain patterns of action. The definition of belief as habit is non-normative in that both true and false beliefs will ground patterns of action. This descriptive status of belief creates a need to incorporate an instrumental criterion in the pragmatic account of truth: a belief vis-à-vis habit can only reasonably be characterized as true if it makes a positive epistemic contribution to the other dimensions of truth, in particular the coherence element. As such, any given pattern of action, X, which has been adopted as a functional response to holding the belief that P, is truth-conducive only if X coheres with the totality of our practical experience.

This interpretation suggests the following instrumental definition of truth: A's belief that P is true insofar as P grounds an effective disposition to adopt a certain course of action, X, such that the consequences of X are conducive to the attainment of A's rational aims and cohere with the totality of A's belief-set. Figure 2.3 shows the conceptual relations involved in the definition.

Peirce and James's differing stance on nominalism has a bearing on their understanding of instrumental truth. Peirce argues in favour of the existence of general properties such as 'redness', 'justice' and 'hardness',

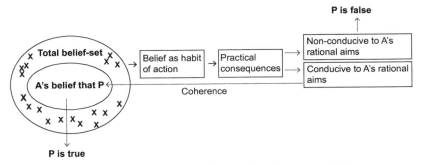

Figure 2.3 Overview of the conceptual relations in the instrumental definition of truth.

whereas James only accepts the actual, particular manifestations of individual instances of events that are 'red', 'just' or 'hard'. As Haack (1976) notes, Peirce addresses <TRUTH> as a metaphysical concepts, whereas James only accepts the existence of individual <truths>.[8] In the following quotes, James (1975b, 32; 30) makes his nominalistic turn of pragmatism quite clear:

> It [pragmatism] agrees with nominalism for instance, in always appealing to particulars. ... There can *be* no difference anywhere that doesn't *make* a difference elsewhere – no difference in abstract truth that doesn't express itself in a difference in concrete fact and in conduct consequent upon that fact, imposed on somebody, somehow, somewhere and somewhen. The whole function of philosophy ought to be to find out what definite difference it will make to you and me, at definite instants of our life, if this world-formula or that world-formula be the true one.

Transferred to an interpretation of the general definition of instrumental truth, the differences between Peirce and James play out as follows:

James' nominalist definition of instrumental truth
A's belief that P is true insofar as P grounds an effective disposition to adopt a certain course of action, X, such that the consequences of X are conducive to the attainment of A's rational aims *in a specific context*, C, and cohere with the totality of A's belief-set.

Peirce's universalist definition of instrumental truth
A's belief that P is true insofar as P *would* ground *in all rational agents*, An, an effective disposition to adopt a certain course of action, X, such that the consequences of X *would be* conducive to the attainment of An's aims and cohere with the totality of *their* belief-set.

James's nominalism gets him into serious trouble. Moore's and Russell's counterargument to the Jamesian interpretation is that if instrumental truth is conditional on practical applicability in individual contexts for individual agents, then subjectivism and relativism are inevitable. What is useful to A may not be useful to B, and, therefore, we end up in the following contradictory situation: (a) the belief that P may produce useful consequences for A_1 in context C, which would turn P true in C; (b) the belief that P may *fail to* produce useful consequences for another agent, A_2, in C, which would turn P false. P may therefore be true and false in the same context.

As discussed, Haack (1976) suggests that James can fight off the objection by making his definition conditional on useful consequences *over time*. The idea is that a true belief would start to produce helpful consequences at some future point in time or, in another formulation of the problem, would manifest itself as coherent with the totality of the agent's belief-set. Likewise, holding on to false beliefs would at some future point in time become counterproductive and decrease the coherence of one's belief-set. While this temporal corrective may significantly decrease the probability of the contradictory scenario, it does not rule it out: there is no guarantee that continued commitment to a false belief will necessarily become counterproductive or incoherent with experience at some future point in time. For this reason, the Peircean definition of instrumental truth is the more coherent one.

2.5 Conclusion

The American pragmatists developed a grand theory of truth, which merges four distinct criteria into a unified framework. Figure 2.4 summarizes the theory. When all four building blocks are tied together, the pragmatic definition of truth goes as follows.

A's belief that P is true when the following four conditions are the case. First, beliefs are behavioural dispositions that ground certain patterns of actions. The correspondence criterion requires a clearly identifiable referential relation between P and the consequences of holding and acting on P. Correspondence is thereby a tracking condition that obtains when it is possible (i) to trace the practical consequences of believing and acting on P, and (ii) to attribute these consequences to the fact that A believes that P. This controversial formulation of the correspondence criteria rests on Peirce's definition of belief as habit. Second, the coherence criterion requires that

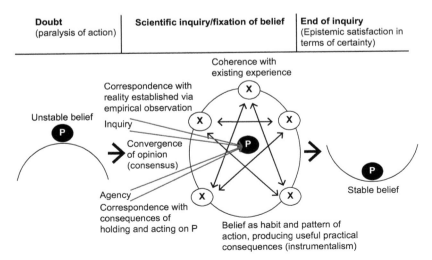

Figure 2.4 Conceptual model of the pragmatic theory of truth.

the consequences of holding and acting on P should cohere with the totality of A's belief-set and practical experience. Third, the consensus criterion calls for inter-subjective agreement on the extent to which holding and acting on P cohere with collective experience and correspond to external reality as established through continued empirical inquiry of P. Finally, the instrumental criterion holds that P needs to manifest itself as an effective behavioural disposition to adopt a certain course of action, X, such that any agent that believes that P would be effectively motivated to do X and doing so would be conducive to their rational aims and cohere with the totality of their belief-set.

Linking back to Peirce's conceptualization of science as a process of stabilizing unsettled beliefs, the process of epistemic justification describes the fixation of an individual belief as it is acted on and corroborated over time.

Notes

1 Peirce discusses the epistemological significance of belief-stabilization in *The Fixation of Belief* (1986, 242–257). I shall return to the topic in Section 2.3.
2 There is a direct link between Peirce's notion of true belief as grounding a successful pattern of action and the instrumental criterion of truth developed in Chapter 5. Leaving details aside, the instrumental criterion holds that a behavioural marketing claim is true insofar as the brand successfully facilitates courses of action that will realize the promised behavioural aim.
3 Metaphysical realism is the view that the external world exists independently of our mind. This view is often associated with causal theories of meaning that condition linguistic meaning on referential relations to external facts. By contrast, metaphysical anti-realism is the view that the external world is constructed by our conception of the world and, consequently, that there is no objective world behind our concepts of the world. This position is usually linked to an epistemic theory of meaning such as the coherence theory. Crossover epistemologies integrate elements of realism and anti-realism and often comprise significant explanatory power. As argued above, my view is that pragmatism is an example of such a crossover epistemology. Influential modern examples include Dummett's semantic anti-realism that assumes the existence of a mind-independent, objective world, but argues that our understanding of the world will always be shaped by our cognitive outlook: truth is a form of warranted assertability. There are striking parallels between Dummett's and Dewey's accounts of truth. Although I shall not explicitly discuss realism/anti-realism with regards to the theory of truth in marketing, it is worth noting that the theory merges elements of both positions given its commitment to the correspondence and coherence theory of truth. Also, the theory's emphasis on both natural and conventional product properties indicates an underpinning commitment to a crossover epistemology (see Chapter 3).
4 Chapter 4, Section 4.5, discusses in detail how the theory of truth in marketing fends off the plurality objection. The problem is solved by controlling the scope of alethic inquiry rather than by reference to beliefs as habits of action. The notion of belief as habit of action primarily influenced the development of the instrumental criterion in Chapter 5.
5 Peirce cited in Haack (1976, 246).

6 Chapter 1 briefly discussed falsificationism in relation to Popper's philosophy of science and argued why the theory of truth in marketing relies on verificationism rather than falsificationism.

7 Peirce and James disagree over pragmatism's stance on verificationism and falsificationism. Contrary to Peirce, James (1975b, 97) expresses a clear commitment to verificationism: *"True ideas are those that we can assimilitate, validate, corroborate and verify. False ideas are those that we cannot."*

8 The theory of truth in marketing is non-nominalist: the core entity in the theory's ontology is the abstract object 'brand' or 'brand universe'. James would insist that there is no such thing as a (truthful) brand, but only particular instances, that is, services and products, in relation to which marketing propositions are true or false. By contrast, Peirce's epistemology allows for the possibility of the abstract notion of a (truthful) brand.

3 The correspondence criterion of truth

> Thus although truth and falsehood are properties of beliefs, yet they are in a sense extrinsic properties, for the condition of the truth of a belief is something not involving beliefs, or (in general) any mind at all, but only the *objects* of the belief. A mind, which believes, believes truly when there is a *corresponding* complex not involving the mind, but only its objects. This correspondence ensures truth, and its absence entails falsehood. ... Thus a belief is true when there is a corresponding fact, and is false when there is no corresponding fact.
>
> Bertrand Russell, *The Problems of Philosophy*

3.1 Correspondence in historic context

Although the correspondence theory of truth is often associated with Aristotle (*Metaphysics* 1011b25), Plato has formulated similar views on the nature of truth in *Cratylos* (385b2) and *Sophist* (263b). Aristotle's thinking on truth as correspondence became predominant through the philosophy of Thomas Aquinas (1225–1274) – one of the most influential medieval thinkers – that merged Aristotelianism and Neoplatonism. In two of Aquinas's major works, *De Veritate* (1954) and *Summa Theologiae* (2006), truth is defined as correspondence between thoughts (intellect) and their objects.[1]

The legacy of the correspondence theory is evident in its significant influence on modern analytical philosophy (Austin 1950; Davidson 1969; Russell 1998; Sellars 1959; Wittgenstein 1971) and contemporary epistemology (Armstrong 2004; Beebee and Dodd 2005b; Bernard and Horgan 2013; Fumerton 2013; Kitcher 2002; López de Sa 2010; Marino 2010; Sher 2013 Wright and Pedersen 2010c).

This theory has played such a predominant role throughout the history of philosophy because it obviously captures something fundamental about the way in which we intuitively think about truth: truth is analyzable in terms of a relation between language and the world (Davidson 1969). The core idea is that if something, X, is true, then that is because X stands in a certain relation to the external world, W. Truth is a relational property between

The correspondence criterion of truth   43

X and W such that X is true to the extent that some entity, x, that belongs to W at some point in time, t, makes X true: X is true at t insofar as W(x) is the case at t. By way of example, a statement like 'The car is parked in the driveway' is true at some point in time, say today at 6.15 pm, insofar as the car is parked in the driveway today at 6.15 pm.[2]

Aristotle puts the idea this way in one of his major works, *Metaphysics* (1011b25) (Kirwan 1971):

> This will be plain if we first define what truth and falsehood are: for to say that that which is is not or that which is not is, is a falsehood; and to say that that which is is and that which is not is not, is true.

In the modern history of philosophy, the correspondence theory of truth came to prominence through the influential works of Russell (1998) and Wittgenstein (1971). Both philosophers developed a form of logical atomism (Klement 2015; Proops 2013), which relies on a correspondence view of truth that substantially improves the historical indeterminacy of the theory's core notion of fact or external reality. According to logical atomism, the world is composed of simple entities – atomic states of affairs – and all propositions are true or false in relation to these atomic facts. An alethic analysis of complex claims and theories thereby amounts to the breaking down of complex propositions into their simpler constituents until one reaches the smallest possible units of meaning: atomic sentences. These atomic sentences are then thought to refer to simple atomic facts in the external world. Complex meaning is thereby a function of logically valid compositions of atomic sentences, and complex truth can be determined by analyzing the logical connections between atomic sentences.

Logical atomism has exercised lasting influence on analytic philosophy, but the position, with its heavy commitment to a realist ontology, came under sustained pressure from anti-realist epistemology. The result was that the correspondence theory of truth lost ground to a plethora of alternate views, such as the coherence theory of truth, truth as warranted assertability, pragmatic truth, and, more recently, deflationism and the identity theory of truth. Today, the correspondence theory of truth enjoys a partial renaissance in alethic pluralism, the view that truth is a multidimensional property that can materialize in different ways and, therefore, calls for a pluralistic theory featuring various criteria of truth (Bernard and Horgan 2013; Fumerton 2013; Lynch 2004, 2009; Sher 2013). Thus, alethic pluralism often employs correspondence as one out a number of truth criteria, as did the American pragmatists. This is indeed also the case with regard to the theory of truth in marketing: as the following chapters will argue, the analysis of truth in marketing must rely on an applied theory of alethic pluralism, in which correspondence is embedded as one out of three criteria of truth.

3.2   The general correspondence theory of truth

As mentioned, the root idea of the correspondence theory is that something is true by virtue of some ontological features in the external, objective world. This motivates the following simple definition of truth:

Generic definition of truth as correspondence
X is true at some point in time, t, insofar as X corresponds to some external entity, x, in the objective world, W, such that $W(x)$ at t.

The definition under-determines three key questions. First, what is the class of semantic entities that can be true or false? Second, what is the class of ontological entities that makes semantic entities true or false? Finally, what does it mean for a semantic entity to correspond to an ontological entity in a way that is constitutive of truth? The first question is about *truth-bearers*; the second question addresses the notion of *truth-makers*; and the last question asks about the nature of the correspondence relation between truth-bearers and truth-makers. I will now briefly address each of the questions in terms of the treatment in pure epistemology, and I will then adapt these core concepts to the domain of truth in marketing.

Truth-bearers and truth-makers

A truth-bearer is a semantic entity that carries some content that can be assessed in terms of truth and falsity (Armstrong 2004; Beebee and Dodd 2005a). Correspondence theorists have proposed a plethora of different candidates for truth-bearers. Kirkham (1992, 54) sums up the variety of suggestions:

> Among the candidates are beliefs, propositions, judgements, assertions, statements, theories, remarks, ideas, acts of thought, utterances, sentence tokens, sentence types, sentences (unspecified), and speech acts.

However, an analysis of the various different suggestions will demonstrate that the fundamental component of truth-bearers is propositional content or, at least, that the candidates are all analyzable in terms of propositional content. The differing candidates may not be entirely reducible to propositional content, but their alethic function is grounded in their propositional content. Even speech acts (understood within Searle's [1969] framework) are propositional in that they communicate messages – warnings, promises, apologies, invitations – which conceptual analysis can break down into propositional constituents. David (2015) distinguishes between two different views on the nature of propositions. On the Fregean view propositions are concepts of objects and their properties and relations. By contrast, the Russellian view holds that propositions are constituted of objects and, thereby, that there is a structural resemblance between the semantic and ontological domains. Truth-makers are some portion of reality, in virtue of which a truth-bearer is true (Armstrong 2004). They are the ontological ground that makes the semantic truth-bearer true or false (Armstrong 1991; Beebee and Dodd 2005a). Truth-makers exist independently of our minds and linguistic constructions, and thereby presuppose a realist ontology. The philosophical literature suggests a number of different truth-maker candidates such as facts, states of affairs, properties, events and situations (David 2015). The most influential proponents prefer facts (Davidson 1969; Russell 1998; Wittgenstein 1971) or states of affairs (Armstrong 1991, 2004). It is difficult to provide a precise account of truth-bearers and truth-makers in isolation from a discussion of what correspondence is because the concepts are tightly interwoven. Any given stance on the nature of truth-bearers and truth-makers is strongly influenced by one's view of the correspondence relation, which will become especially apparent when we come to the discussion of isomorphism.

It is paramount to be aware of one crucial difference between facts and states of affairs in their capacity of truth-makers. Their ontological status differs, and this has implications for the domain of truths over which the correspondence theory can range. A fact is something that is the case, and, thereby, facts have *actual* existence (David 2005). By contrast, the notion of states of affairs under-determines existence and thereby may express *potentiality*.[3] This is important because some truths are made true by potential circumstances. Of particular importance are counterfactual conditionals, which are true in terms of merely possible states of affairs.[4] For example, a sentence like 'If you hadn't pressed the brake pedal hard, you would have hit the child' is true in terms of a potential scenario, which did not obtain. To exclusively define truth-makers as facts thereby implies either that one cannot account for counterfactual truths, or the assumption that potential scenarios have existence of some sort. The former consequent compromises explanatory power, whereas the latter consequent requires the adoption of non-intuitive metaphysical assumptions that are difficult to justify. Although an exhaustive theory of truth in marketing would have to incorporate counterfactual truths and thereby work with both facts and state of affairs as truth-makers, the marketing specific criterion of correspondence to be developed will only focus on factual and conditional truths.[5]

The correspondence relation between truth-bearers and truth-makers

The most challenging part of the correspondence theory is to specify the alethic relation between truth-bearers and truth-makers. Not surprisingly, throughout the theory's history, the exact nature of the relation has often been left under-determined. Three accounts of correspondence are central: isomorphism; correlation; and cross-categorial entailment.

Isomorphism

The early Wittgenstein (1971) provided a seminal attempt to flesh out the correspondence relation in terms of isomorphism in his groundbreaking work *Tractatus Logico-Philosophicus*. As indicated in the short description of logical atomism above, Wittgenstein conceptualizes truth as a relation between two separate domains – a semantic and an ontological realm – which at some level of analysis share the same structure: language and external reality are isomorphs. The isomorphic properties of the differing domains are their logical structure.

All complex objects in the external world are combinations of simpler objects, which ultimately are comprised of atomic facts. Atomic facts are the minimal and essential unit of analysis and thereby function as truth-makers. As external reality, language comprises complex semantic structures, which can be analyzed into simpler units of meaning until one reaches the ultimate semantic ground: atomic sentences, which copy atomic facts. And it is precisely by virtue of this particular capacity of language to copy the external world or picture atomic facts that propositional statements are true or false. Atomic sentences are thereby truth-bearers.

In general, the isomorphic view can be summarized as follows: When the relation, R, between a fact, f, and a proposition, P, is such that both f and P share the same logical structure, S, then R becomes an alethic correspondence relation between P and f given S. Isomorphic approaches have to define truth-makers as facts rather than properties because it is difficult to see how a proposition can share the same structure as a physical property. For example, how can the proposition 'The car is red' have the same alethic structure as the corresponding property 'redness'? Isomorphism then has to provide a convincing account of facts as something that is somehow embedded in ontological entities, whilst not being part of their physical properties or relations. This is no easy challenge.

Correlation

Indeed, the argument in favor of the competing view of correspondence as correlation is motivated by the lack of a convincing account of genuine isomorphism. Austin (1950, 119) comments:

> There is no need whatsoever for the words used in making a true statement to "mirror" in any way, however indirect, any feature whatsoever of the situation or event; a statement no more needs, in order to be true, to reproduce the "multiplicity," say, or the "structure" or "form" of the reality, than a word needs to be echoic or writing pictographic. To suppose that it does, is to fall once again into the error of reading back into the world the features of language.

According to Austin, isomorphism fails because it projects the structure of language onto reality. In order to make isomorphism work, the proponents have to adopt a definition of truth-makers that come at considerable metaphysical costs: reality is defined in order to fit the semantic categories of language. This move seems to run counter to the pre-theoretic plausibility of the correspondence theory; that is, it intuitively catches our understanding of truth as a relation between language and a mind-independent world. A related argument is that 'language' and 'world' do not comprise two separate domains connected via a correspondence relation. Our experience of the world is fundamentally linguistic in the sense that we cannot, conceptually speaking, experience the world independently of the categories of language. Our view of the world is necessarily shaped by the semantic structure of language.

To address these challenges, Austin proposes a novel view of correspondence, which puts conventions centre stage. A proposition (truth-bearer) is correlated with entities in the external world (truth-maker) by means of linguistic convention. Austin distinguishes between two types of alethically relevant conventions. First, descriptive conventions *correlate* words (propositions) with specific *types* of things in the external world. For example, the sentence 'The car is red' correlates with a certain type of situation that exemplifies what we, by convention, define as being a red car. Second, demonstrative conventions *correlate* propositions with historic situations, that is, particular instances of a given state of affairs. For example, the sentence 'The car is red' addresses a specific car at a specific point in time. Austin defines truth as the correct correlation between demonstrative and descriptive conventions such that a sentence is true insofar as the historic situation correlates to what we by convention define as being a car and being red.[6] Figure 3.1 illustrates my interpretation of Austin's idea of correspondence as conventional correlation.

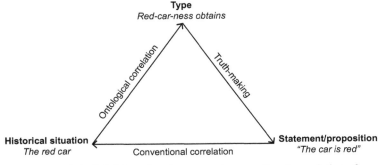

Figure 3.1 Austin's definition of truth as correct conventional correlation of statements (propositions) to their external referents in the objective world.

Austin refuses to take a metaphysical stance on realism versus anti-realism and therefore would not agree with Figure 3.1's conceptualization of the relation between the historical situation and the type as an ontological correlation. His claim is that philosophical problems are linguistic in the sense that a correct analysis and understanding of the way in which humans use natural languages will solve – or make irrelevant – the majority of traditional philosophical problems. But, as Kirkham (1992) notes, Austin's view of reality commits him to assuming that truth-makers are mind-independent entities and, accordingly, that his theory of truth rests on a realist ontology. In effect, Austin advocates a common-sense view of reality, suggesting that the correlation between statements and states of affairs is a dual conventional-ontological one.

Cross-categorial necessitation

Armstrong (2004) has contributed a major reconceptualization of the correspondence relation as 'cross-categorial necessitation'. This conceptual invention has sparked much interest in contemporary theory development (David 2005). Armstrong's idea is that truth-makers necessitate the truth of certain propositions, but since these truth-makers are objective states of affairs in the external world, necessitation is not a form of entailment. Here, the necessitation-relation between truth-bearer and truth-maker is *ontological* rather than *semantic* or *deductive*. Armstrong (2004, 5–6) says:

> [T]he first thing to notice is that the necessitation cannot be any form of entailment. Both terms of an entailment relation must be propositions, but the truthmaking term of the truthmaking relation is a portion of reality, and, in general at least, portions of reality are not propositions. The simplest of all truthmaking relations is that which holds between any truthmaker, T, which is something in the world, and the proposition.[7]

On this view, certain configurations of reality necessitate the truth or falsity of statements about the world. Thus, the existence of a red car, C, in a given car park, X, at time t, necessitates the truth of the statement 'There was a red car in X car park at t'. Truth-making is thereby an alethic relation that cuts across the linguistic and ontologic domains and necessitates truths in the former.

The notion of cross-categorial necessitation will inform the development of the marketing-specific criterion of correspondence. I will therefore point out one substantial problem with Armstrong's theory and suggest an obvious corrective. Armstrong defines the alethic correspondence relation in terms of existence: The existence of X (e.g., a red car X) necessitates the truth of Y (e.g., the proposition 'Car X is red'). The insistence on ontological necessitation rather than necessitation by intrinsic properties puts Armstrong into trouble. Assume that car X is red at t_1, but has been painted black at t_2. Accordingly, at t_1 the proposition 'Car X is red' is true, but obviously false at t_2. However, Armstrong cannot explain or accommodate this obvious fact because the car has not changed existence: ontologically speaking, the car is the same; it has just changed colour. But since it is not the intrinsic property 'red' that explains the alethic relation and makes the statement 'Car X is red' true, but rather the existence of the red car, then Armstrong has to hold that the car is no longer the same at t_1 and t_2. Otherwise it would turn the now false statement 'Car X is red' true, which is obviously absurd. The solution to the problem, I will suggest, is to operate with intrinsic properties rather than existence as truth-makers. This solution works because – as we have just seen – intrinsic properties are not essential: an entity can change some intrinsic properties and still remain the same entity.

3.3 Marketing-specific truth-makers and functional claims

The following sections will develop a marketing-specific criterion of correspondence. The purpose of this criterion is to provide a platform from which the truth of functional claims can be assessed. A functional claim is defined by two main characteristics. First, it is a propositional statement in any verbal or visual form holding that a product or service has one or more properties. Second, the veracity of the statement can be determined with reference to natural or social facts. The product or service properties may be physically integrated in the product, materialize during normal usage via consumer-product interactions or be embedded in social conventions. This definition of functional claim establishes a strong linkage to the core explanatory constructs of truth-makers and truth-bearers in the correspondence theory. On the one hand, a functional claim makes a statement about what is or is not the case regarding a given product or service and thereby performs the role of truth-bearer. On the other, product or service properties turn the functional claim true or false and thereby act as truth-maker (fact).

The application of the correspondence criterion to the marketing domain is not without its challenges. A core feature of all of the reviewed correspondence theories is the commitment to a realist ontology, necessitated by the conceptualization of truth-makers as mind-independent entities. However, marketing is neither an objective science nor a domain of non-normative practice, but an intensely eclectic societal phenomenon. Functional claims in the marketing sphere are not limited to objective, external features, and the application of the correspondence criterion will thereby run against the strong realist assumptions by also operating with anti-realist truth-makers that do not exist independently of the mind. To accommodate the heterogeneous nature of marketing practice, it is necessary to cut across the distinction between realism and anti-realism, empiricism and constructivism, and assume the existence of the following two different types of truth-makers: natural and social facts.

Natural Facts

For the purposes of this study, natural facts are properties that are integrated in the core product or service. They come in two different types, that is, inherent properties and supervenient properties.

Inherent properties

These are features that belong to the product or service such that the product or service has the relevant properties independently of any connection with the consumer. Obvious examples are colour, shape, size and material composition. But a range of basic product and service features are also inherent, such as your phone's ability to connect to the Internet via 4G, send texts and make Skype calls.[8] Although these features are only actualized via consumption, their existence is not dependent on you or any other consumer; these features belong to the product. Two important qualifications should be noted. First, product-inherent properties are time-bound in that they have limited duration over time. For example, the quality of a meat-product is highly limited to a specified time-section, whereas the quality of other food products such as salt and sugar remains stable over significant time-sections. Second, context-sensitivity is crucial because some features may belong intrinsically to a product or service but under specified external circumstances only. The examples are abundant: your phone may not work below certain temperatures; the paint in the tin will only cover a certain area of the wall if used in conjunction with a specific roller; your sleeping bag will keep you warm on your camping holiday down to +5° degrees Celsius.

Taking into account the constraints of time-boundedness and context-sensitivity, I define product-inherent properties as follows: a given property, x, belongs inherently to a product, Z, insofar as $Z(x)$ holds within a specified time-section, t_1-t_n, in a certain context, C, independently from any consumer interaction with $Z(x)$ in C at t_1-t_n.

We now know what should be meant by the notion of inherent properties and that these properties are assumed to work as one type of truth-maker for functional marketing claims. But what characterizes the correspondence relation between the properties (truth-makers) and the functional claims (truth-bearers)? Armstrong's notion of cross-categorial necessitation conceptualizes the alethic relation quite well. Applied to this context, the idea would be that a given product, Z, has certain core properties, x, which entail the truth of at least one functional product claim, that is, $Z(x)$. A simple example will prove useful: A bottle of still water is a product that contains a given amount of the physical composition H_2O. This means that the product property H_2O necessitates the truth of the product claim 'Contains water'. The alethic necessitation is cross-categorial in the sense that it is the presence of a physical structure or natural kind (water) that entails the

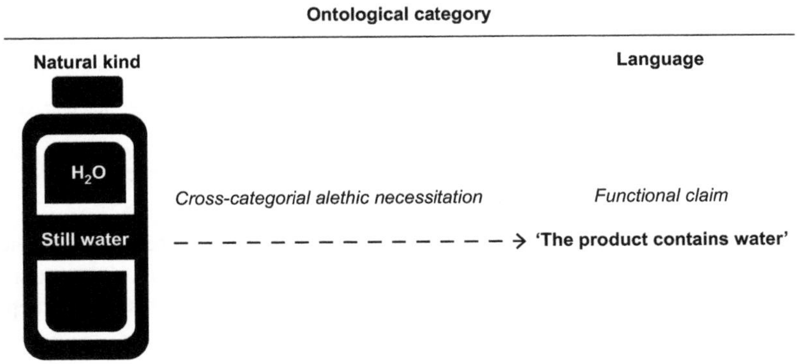

Ontological category

Natural kind	Language

H_2O

Still water

Cross-categorial alethic necessitation   Functional claim

$---------------- \rightarrow$ 'The product contains water'

Figure 3.2 Armstrong's concept of cross-categorial alethic necessitation applied to functional claims in marketing.

necessity of a certain epistemic formation (truth) in a different structure of another kind (language). Figure 3.2 illustrates the process of cross-categorial necessitation.

The discussion of natural facts and inherent properties motivates the following criterion of truth:

Natural fact truth-maker: inherent properties
An inherent property, x, belonging to a specific product/service, Z, is a truth-maker for a functional marketing claim, P, when it is the case that the truth of a specific claim, $P(x)$, is necessitated by the composition of the product/service, $Z(x)$.

Supervenience

Let me now turn to supervenient properties. The standard definition of supervenience holds that a set of properties, P_1, supervenes on a another set of properties, P_2, insofar as any change in the composition of P_2 would lead to a change in the composition of P_1 (McLaughlin and Bennett 2014). The previous example with the sleeping bag can easily be changed to demonstrate the importance of supervenience.

Although most consumers may find that product Z has x feature under C circumstances (e.g., the sleeping bag is comfortably warm at 5° Celsius), some users may find that Z does *not* have x in C (e.g., the sleeping bag is feeling cold at 5° Celsius). The core product property of keeping users warm supervenes on the actual composition of the product and the subjective perception or response of the consumer. I suggest the following marketing-specific definition of product property supervenience: property-supervenience occurs when the core property, x, of a given product, Z, is

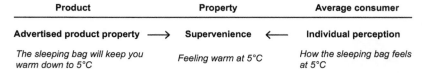

Figure 3.3 Model of the emergence of supervenient product properties.

both product- and subject-dependent such that $Z(x)$ is the case insofar as the user experiences x in terms of her subjective response to Z in a relevant context of consumption. The model shown in Figure 3.3 illustrates the concept of supervenience in marketing.

Supervenience poses a problem in terms of developing a general and operational theory of truth in marketing because the phenomenon introduces subject-dependency. Where context-dependency is a variable that is easily workable within the theoretical framework given that it will apply to all consumers in the same context, the concept of subject-dependency implicit in this form of supervenience means that truth becomes relative to the individual consumer. To continue with the sleeping bag example, there is no general truth pertaining to the thermal properties of the product as these are ultimately relative to the individual consumer. A practical way to tackle this challenge is to make the alethic properties conditional on average, normal or intended consumption.[9] That solution translates subject-dependency into a form of context-dependency, allowing for subjective perception to play a pivotal role, but in the objectified form of 'average subjective experience'.

Supervenient product properties demonstrate why it is not viable to invoke the distinctions between realism and objectivism, on the one hand, and anti-realism and subjectivism, on the other hand. Supervenience grounded in average or intended consumption shows that some product properties are neither inherent features of the product nor subjective constructs in the mind of the consumer, but a phenomenon that emerges across the distinction between objective and subjective, internal and external, realism and constructivism.[10]

The discussion of supervenient product/service properties motivates the following truth-maker definition:

Natural fact truth-maker: supervenient properties

A supervenient property, x, belonging to a given product/service, Z, is a truth-maker for a functional marketing claim, P, when it is the case that the truth of a specific claim, $P(x)$, is necessitated by the average consumer experience of the product/service, $Z(x)$.

Natural facts in the marketing domain

These definitions possesses considerable explanatory power. A recent ASA (2012c) ruling demonstrates how natural fact truth-makers are used to justify alethic decisions in the marketing domain. A company website for the insect repellent, Incognito, stated that the product "provides 100% protection against mosquitoes" and that it "works against all insects! Anywhere in the world". The ASA received a complaint that challenged whether these claims could be substantiated. To justify their ad, Incognito provided a number of scientific studies and test results, which they argued substantiated the claims. But the ASA (2012c) were not impressed, as the following quote shows.

> However, we understood that a significant number of species of mosquito existed and that the advertised product had only been tested on a limited number of those species. We therefore considered the evidence provided was not adequate to substantiate the claim that the advertised product provided 100% protection against mosquitoes they [consumers] might encounter, as the ad implied.

The ruling clearly uses product-inherent properties as truth-makers, and the epistemic access to the truth-makers is established via direct reference to and use of empirical evidence obtained in laboratory tests. But the ruling is not just occupied with the functionality of the product-inherent properties, it also takes into account that the properties of the products are influenced by consumer–product interaction and thereby implicitly addresses the importance of supervenience. This is evident from an analysis of the following part of the ASA ruling.

> We considered consumers would expect the advertised product to provide 100% protection against mosquitoes for the duration Incognito advised when using the product, as per the instructions. The third test report did not make clear whether the dosage used during the test reflected the dosage that consumers would apply when using the advertised product. The "How to use incognito® natural insect repellent products" stated "On average incognito® natural insect repellent spray will give you up to 5 hours of good protection". In that context, we considered consumers would expect the advertised product to provide 100% protection against mosquitoes for a period of up to 5 hours. We were therefore concerned that the study showed that an hour after the test substance had been applied, the product did not provide 100% protection against the mosquitoes tested; rather it provided a significantly lower level of protection.

The core product property – protection against insect bites – behaves as a supervenient property because it emerges as a combined consequence of product-inherent properties (i.e., the chemical formulation of the product) and the variable dosage as administered by the consumer. Incognito's response also follows my previous observation that reference to average consumption would be the obvious way to address the alethic challenges posed by supervenience. Again, the ASA refers to an empirical study to settle the truthfulness of the supervenient property claim. Thus, supervenient and inherent properties work as real-life truth-makers in the marketing domain.

Social facts

The notion of natural fact (inherent and supervenient properties) cannot accommodate all alethically relevant product and service properties. Some essential properties are grounded in social facts. The concept of social fact has a long intellectual history[11] and dates back to Emile Durkheim's seminal treatment of the subject in *The Rules of Sociological Method* first published in 1895. Durkheim (1858–1917) famously put social facts at the core of the emerging discipline of sociology. He defined social facts as empirically observable things that exist independently of individual social agents. But what sort of thing is a social fact? It is a social convention that comprises ways of acting embedded in a social practice via past traditions. These conventional ways of acting set down by past behaviour in a given social group constrain actual and future agency such that individuals acting within the same context pertaining to the convention will feel a social pressure, if they act contrary to the convention. Durkheim (1982, 52) writes:

> Here, then, is a category of facts which present very special characteristics: they consist of manners of acting, thinking and feeling external to the individual, which are invested with a coercive power by virtue of which they exercise control over him. ... Thus they constitute a new species and to them must be exclusively assigned the term *social*.

The concept of social fact relevant to the study of truth in marketing is substantially different from Durkheim's classical formulation. In this context, the unit of analysis is not patterns of behaviour as shaped by and unfolding in society, but alethic properties. We therefore need a social epistemological definition of social fact. Accordingly, let social facts be properties, which belong to a product or service by means of convention. At first, it may seem odd to think of core product features as constructs of convention, but the following examples demonstrate the existence and relevance of conventional properties.

One type of conventional properties of particular importance to marketing is process-based properties, which refer to the conditions under which a certain product has been produced. For example, animal food products may be endorsed by animal welfare charities based on the living conditions of the animals (e.g., free-range eggs); teas and coffees may be labeled fair trade based on the working conditions of the farmers and workers; cotton-based clothing may be labeled organic due to the farming methods used on the cotton fields. But other types of conventional properties are also of relevance to marketing. To take just one more example, what could be called 'professional properties' are attributed to a range of service products, and these properties are fundamental in modern societies as they cover all types of regulated professional agency. Educational degrees are an obvious example as they often entitle candidates to become members of a chartered organization (e.g., chartered psychologists, accountants or engineers). This conventional, augmented property is a defining characteristic of the product because it enables the owner to exercise her profession.

There is potentially a long list of different types of conventional properties in marketing. This is not of any concern here. What is needed for our purposes is to spell out the defining characteristics of conventional properties in marketing. The examples discussed in this chapter indicate that a conventional property is established by means of a designated set of people who have the power to endorse a product in a particular respect and confer a certain type of value to the product. Accordingly, let all conventional properties be authoritative social constructs such that for any given conventional property, CP, there is an epistemically privileged group of professionals that (a) define the characteristics, x, of CP, (b) specify the conditions under which $CP(x)$ obtains, and (c) in some cases determine the range of actions that $CP(x)$ allows its owner to perform.[12] The model presented in Figure 3.4 illustrates the nature of conventional product properties.

Social facts as truth-makers

On the face of it, it seems that the coherence criterion of truth would do a much better job of explaining the alethic dimension of social facts than, as I will suggest, the correspondence criterion. The observation driving this objection is that social facts here are epistemic entities that are linked to other epistemic entities (e.g., certifying or professional bodies), which specify the ontological and semantic dimension of the social facts (i.e., when do they obtain; what do they mean; which courses of action do they entitle the

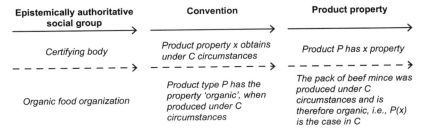

Epistemically authoritative social group	Convention	Product property
Certifying body	Product property x obtains under C circumstances	Product P has x property
Organic food organization	Product type P has the property 'organic', when produced under C circumstances	The pack of beef mince was produced under C circumstances and is therefore organic, i.e., P(x) is the case in C

Figure 3.4 The emergence of conventional product properties.

owner to perform). The relevant alethic relation seems to be some type of epistemic justification between epistemic entities. And this is precisely the hallmark of coherence.

There are two reasons why I insist on applying the correspondence criterion to accommodate the truth of conventional properties in marketing. The first reason is that Austin's reformulation of the correspondence theory builds on truth as being partly constituted by means of convention. We saw how in Austin's work social conventions correlate statements (propositions) with historical situations (facts, states of affairs), which are then ontologically correlated with relevant types or general exemplars that act as truth-makers. Mapping Austin's alethic schema loosely onto our case of truth in marketing, we can say that claims about conventional properties refer to social facts (social situations), which are then ontologically correlated to epistemically privileged sets of agents that determine the relevant types of conditions under which the social facts obtain and thereby act as truth-makers.

This argument does not demonstrate that the coherence criterion is unable to accommodate social facts. What it does show is that correspondence and coherence are competing explanatory criteria. However, as I will now explain, correspondence not only has the competitive edge over coherence with respect to social facts, but is the only real candidate because there is one aspect of the alethic dimension of conventional properties that the coherence criterion cannot easily work with. Although of a special type, we are very clearly dealing with external truth-makers. Insofar as conventional properties are social constructs, the materialization of which is defined by an external entity (i.e., a designated group of epistemically privileged people), then that external reality acts as truth-maker. The structure of truth is thereby identical to the core idea underpinning the correspondence theory of truth, namely, that truth is a correlation between a claim about an alleged fact (in this case, a conventional property) and the existence of that fact. What makes this a special case is that the fact is social rather than natural, and it is constituted through social agency rather than by means of types, general exemplars or natural processes governed by the laws of nature.

Against this background, I suggest the following definition of truth with respect to social facts.

Social fact truth-maker

A conventional property, x, belonging to a specific product/service, Z, is a truth-maker for a functional marketing claim, P, when it is the case that the truth of a specific claim, $P(x)$, is warranted by its correlation to a set of social conventions that specify the conditions under which $Z(x)$ obtains as defined by an epistemically privileged set of people.

Social facts in the marketing domain

Compared to natural facts, social facts may play a less predominant alethic role in marketing. Social facts (in the form of conventional product properties) are nevertheless employed to settle the truthfulness of factual marketing claims in mainstream cases. Social fact truth-making is not an exception to the rule; rather, it is an integral part of a comprehensive exposition of truth in marketing. The following ASA (2010) adjudication is an example.

Yoga Alliance, a UK company that provides yoga classes and training for yoga instructors, bought two magazine ads, which claimed that the company provided professional standards. The ad copy read: "Yoga Alliance UK Setting Standards for Yoga in the UK". A competing yoga provider, The British Wheel of Yoga, charged that the ad was misleading because Yoga Alliance was not in a position to set any authoritative professional standards in the industry. The adjudicator responded:

> The ASA understood that it was the role of Sport England, a nondepartmental public body under the Department for Culture, Media and Sport, to create a community sport system by working with the national governing bodies of sport. We noted that BWY [The British Wheel of Yoga] was recognised by Sport England as the national governing body of yoga.

Based on the fact that Yoga Alliance was *not* recognized by Sport England as the national governing body of yoga, the ASA ruled the ad to be misleading and unsubstantiated.

This adjudication is a clear-cut example of social facts (conventional properties) being used as truth-makers, and accordingly, it also mirrors Austin's theory of correspondence as a conventional alethic correlation. The explanation is as follows. Yoga Alliance held that it was setting professional standards. This claim referred to an alleged conventional property (social fact), that is, the assumed actual professional standards of yoga instruction. The existence and nature of this conventional property, however, were determined by other social actors, that is, an epistemically privileged group of people (a professional subgroup of Sport England). Mapping this situation onto the definition of social fact truth-making, we have the following situation. The individual agent, A, makes the factual claim $P(x)$ where x is a conventional property/social fact. The privileged epistemic agent, B, defines the conventional conditions, CC, under which x obtains. According to B's definition of CC, x does not obtain under the circumstances specified by A's claim $P(x)$ and the claim is therefore false.

3.4   Objections

Given the long history and significant influence of the correspondence theory of truth, it is not surprising that it has been subject to severe criticism. This section discusses two of the core challenges regarding the essential concept of 'fact' and provides solutions that are specific to the marketing context.

On falsehood and non-existent facts

White (1971) argues that the correspondence theory of truth is committed to an unreasonable account of facts. Both natural and formal languages operate with disjunctive, conditional and negative statements, and in both cases these statements share the fundamental alethic feature with descriptive sentences that they can be true or false. If truth is expressed in terms of a correspondence relation between propositions (language) and external reality (facts), then the correspondence theorist has to assume the existence of disjunctive, conditional and negative facts. But this is an unreasonable assumption because what is conditional, disjunctive or negative does not have any actual existence and thereby cannot be a fact. To paraphrase Aristotle: what is not is not.

The proposed problem regarding disjunctive and conditional facts is of less concern as a convincing account of potentiality should do away with this part of the objection. The problem of negative facts is more challenging as we do not have a convincing modus of existence that can explain the ontological status of negative facts. Indeed, Williams (1976) argues that the problem with the correspondence theory is its struggling attempts to explain – not truth – but falsehoods. If truth is expressed in terms of a correspondence relation between a proposition, P, and an objective fact, x, then the claim $P(x)$ is true insofar as $P(x)$ corresponds to x. Conversely, if $P(x)$ is false, then it is so in virtue of its reference to not-$P(x)$. But this is absurd as not-$P(x)$ is a non-entity without existence: claims cannot refer to things that do not exist.

The underpinning assumption that motivates the objection is that truth and falsehood require ontological existence. Obviously, in a semantic-logical sense, this assumption is false as truth is a function of the relation between premises and conclusions, independently of whether the actual content of the premises is true or false in the real world (Forbes 1994). But the point here is that we are after truth as a relation between language and reality and therefore have to produce a theory that explains how the existence of non-existent facts can explain falsehoods. But why should we buy into this argument in the first place?

One can reasonably challenge whether true and false claims are necessarily of the same form. It is perfectly possible to define true claims as referential statements that relate language to natural or social facts, and at the same time to define false claims as non-referential statements where no such relation obtains. On this account, we do not need to postulate any form of quasi-existence of negative facts because false sentences simply do not refer to anything in the external world. Relational language-to-world-reference is a unique characteristic of true statements.

This response to the objection also explains falsehoods in marketing. The previously discussed example with yoga standards is a good case in point. To recall, Yoga Alliance claimed that it was setting professional standards for yoga trainers. This claim was challenged by a competing yoga organization, and the ASA upheld the complaint on the grounds that Yoga Alliance was not recognized by Sport England. This decision can be easily expressed in terms of falsehood being a statement with an empty reference. Yoga Alliance's claim did *not* correspond to the official standards specified by the epistemically privileged agents (Sport England) because it failed to establish a referential relation between language and external social reality. Consequently, there is no need to postulate the existence of a non-fact (i.e., the existence of the absence of official yoga standards referred to by Yoga Alliance).

Fact skepticism

There is no such thing as a fact. Or, at least, there is no epistemically relevant notion of fact. This is a view proposed by a number of opponents to the correspondence theory (Davidson 1990; Lewis 1946; Strawson 1950).[13] If it is substantiated, it derails the correspondence theory because facts (or another functionally identical concept such as states of affairs or events) play the pivotal truth-making role. The correspondence theory simply cannot get off the ground if it does not have a compelling account of fact. The marketing-specific correspondence criterion is indeed founded on the concepts of natural and social facts. Let us have a closer look at why the ontological status and epistemic relevance of facts is called into question.

Here is Davidson's (1990, 303–304) critique, which sums up the general dissatisfaction with the fact concept:[14]

> The real objection to correspondence theories is simpler; it is that there is nothing interesting or instructive to which true sentences might correspond. The point was made some time ago by C. I. Lewis; he challenged the correspondence theorist to locate the fact or part of reality, or of the world, to which a true sentence corresponded. One can locate individual objects, if the sentence happens to name or describe them, but even such location makes sense relative only to a frame of reference, and so presumably the frame of reference must be included in whatever it is to which a true sentence corresponds.

Following out this line of thought led Lewis to conclude that, if true sentences correspond to anything at all, it must be the universe as a whole; thus, all true sentences correspond to the same thing. ... The correct objection to correspondence theories is not, then, that they make truth something to which humans can never legitimately aspire; the real objection is rather that such theories fail to provide entities to which truth vehicles (whether we take these to be statements, sentences or utterances) can be said to correspond.

The crux of the matter is that correspondence theorists are unable to specify what it means for a fact to exist. Should they succeed, then another problem appears, namely, that any individual fact will be part of a referential framework, which means that it is not the individual fact – but the framework of facts – that makes individual claims about the world true. The absurd consequence is that the referent for individual sentences becomes the entire world as such. Contrary to this objection, I will argue that it is possible to clearly identify and locate facts, and thereby truth-makers, in marketing (and, by inference, other applied domains).

Natural facts are unproblematic because they exist as actual properties embedded in products and services and it is possible, by empirical means, to observe these properties and thereby establish the veracity of relevant functional claims. In this case, it is difficult to see how one can convincingly advance Davidson's claim that there is nothing to which functional marketing claims correspond because the alethic properties evidently exist and are readily identifiable and verifiable. But what about social facts? Surely, Lewis and Davidson would object that it is impossible to locate them empirically and that social facts therefore cannot be truth vehicles. I disagree.

Social facts are conventional properties that belong to a product or service by means of an epistemically authoritative group of people assigning a specific value to the product or service. Conventional facts are thereby social constructions, and their emergence is clearly located in this authoritative group of people. For example, when a person obtains a driving license, the crucial product feature of having obtained the legal right to drive is a conventional property, which exists by means of a legal body specifying certain conditions that must obtain in order for a person to be allowed to drive. Likewise, when a pack of beef mince holds the property 'organic', this is again a conventional property that is attributed to the product by means of meeting certain standards of production defined by a certifying organization – that is, an epistemically authoritative social group. Two things stand out about social facts. First, they are social constructs whose actual existence is easily located in individual products and services as conventional properties. Second, their ontological status is clear and unproblematic: it is an identifiable social group with epistemic command that defines the conditions under which social facts obtain. Again, the concern that the correspondence theory is doomed to fail to provide entities to which truth-bearers should correspond is unfounded: the actual existence and emergence of social facts/conventional properties is fully accounted for in the theory of truth in marketing.

3.5 Conclusion

A functional marketing claim holds that a product or service has certain properties. This chapter developed an alethic correspondence criterion that defines what it is for a functional claim to be true. Roughly, a functional marketing claim, P, that a product has a certain property, x, is true insofar as the relevant product or service has that property such that $P(x)$ is the case. This means that functional claims are truth-bearers and product and service properties are the corresponding truth-makers that turn the claims true or false. To explore this broad idea in greater detail, I introduced the distinction between natural and social facts.

On the one hand, I conceptualized natural facts as either product/service inherent properties or supervenient properties. The truth of a claim referring to inherent properties turned out to be a matter of cross-categorial necessitation such that the composition of the product or service necessitates the truth of that claim. The truth of a claim referring to supervenient properties

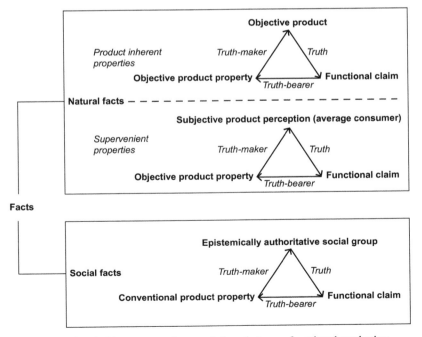

Figure 3.5 The alethic correspondence relations between functional marketing claims (truth-bearers) and natural and social facts (truth-makers).

was defined in terms of a correlation between the composition of the product and the subjective perception of the average consumer.

On the other hand, social facts were defined as conventional properties that belong to products or services in virtue of authoritative epistemic agents assigning particular properties to these products or services. The truth of a claim referring to conventional properties was then defined in terms of its correlation to the conditions under which the properties obtain as defined by the relevant authoritative epistemic agents. Figure 3.5 summarizes this chapter's attempt to develop a marketing-specific correspondence criterion to establish the truth of functional claims.

Notes

1 The often-cited Latin phrase goes: "Veritas est adaequatio rei et intellectus".
2 Descartes (1991, 139) comments on the obviousness of some variant of the correspondence theory: "I have never had any doubts about truth, because it seems a notion so transcendentally clear that nobody can be ignorant of it. ... the word 'truth', in the strict sense, denotes the conformity of thought with its object." As we shall see, however, the correspondence theory is deceptively complex and open to a wide range of different interpretations. Employing the theory in applied domains further requires a number of complex adaptations, in particular of the associated concept of truth-makers.
3 It is important to be precise about the usage of the terms 'facts' and 'states of affairs', given the considerable terminological disagreement and confusion over the concepts. For example, Armstrong (2004) prefers the term 'states of affairs' to 'facts', but his definition of states of affairs as circumstances that necessarily obtain reduces the concept to facts (David 2005).
4 Following Goodman's (1947) seminal article on counterfactuals, the topic has played a predominant role in mainstream epistemology and modal logic (Hendricks 2006). Counterfactuals are subjunctive conditionals of the following syntactic form: 'if X had been the case, then Y would have been the case'. Lewis (1973) and Stalnaker (1968) have defined the truth of counterfactuals in terms of possible world semantics. Roughly, the idea is that a counterfactual conditional 'if X were the case, then Y would be the case' is true insofar as X is true in a possible world, W_1, *and* Y is true in another possible world, W_2, which is *closer* to W_1 than any other world, Wn, where Y is false. The notion of 'closeness of worlds' is crucial and is classically defined in terms of a similarity relation (Lewis 1973; Nute 1975, Stalnaker 1968).
5 Counterfactuals are often not particularly obvious in marketing communications, but nonetheless rather important: informative marketing communications such as terms and conditions may feature counterfactuals. For example, the mandatory information included with consumer credit agreements may state something along the lines: 'based on the assumption that you had borrowed £1,000 under the Agreement, the total amount payable would have been £1.300.' This exploration will not analyze the alethic properties of counterfactual marketing claims in any detail because they represent a highly specialized type of functional marketing claims. The focus here is the truth conditions of functional, symbolic and behavioural claims at a generic level.
6 Austin's (1950, 116) definition of truth goes like this: "A statement is said to be true when the historic state of affairs to which it is correlated by the

demonstrative conventions (the one to which it "refers") is of a type with which the sentence used in making it is correlated by the descriptive conventions".

7 Note that in this quote Armstrong explicitly holds that the necessitation-relation cannot be a form of entailment. However, he frequently refers to this relation as a form of ontological entailment (Armstrong 1997). This observation is consistent with influential interpretations of Armstrong's view (David 2005).

8 Some may object that services cannot have any inherent properties because consumer value and thereby service properties are co-created in the interaction between the brand or service and the consumer (Grönroos 2011; Grönroos and Voima 2013; Vargo and Lusch 2004). The following qualification solves the issue: a service-inherent property, x, belongs to a service, S, if S promises that the consumer, C, will have access to x insofar as C purchases S. This holds even though P will only be actualized via C's interaction with the service provider. The following example demonstrates the point: when a student pays a tuition fee, she effectively buys a service. Although the ultimate service product – the degree – is indeed based on active consumer co-creation, the basic service (i.e., the educational programme) comes with a number of inherent features such as access to lectures, supervision, libraries and exams. These properties are not based on co-creation, but are inherent service properties.

9 The relationship between truth and supervenience has attracted some attention in relation to truth-maker theory (Armstrong 2004; Dodd 2002). Bigelow (1988), for instance, argues that truth supervenes on being. However, our interest in supervenience is different. The extant philosophical discussion centres on the question of whether truth as such is a supervenient phenomenon. By contrast, here is the focus on the truth of claims about supervenient properties.

10 The exposition of truth as a middle position between realism and anti-realism, subjectivism and objectivism, resonates with constructive realism in the social (Cupchik 2001) and political (Lebow 2004) sciences, but is substantially different from constructive realism/empiricism in the philosophy of science (Giere 1985; van Fraassen 1980).

11 See Gilbert's (1989) *On Social Facts* for a comprehensive philosophical discussion of the nature of social fact.

12 Not surprisingly, the highly specialized use of the concept of social convention is markedly different from Austin or Durkheim's view of conventions. On their view, a convention is *historical* in the sense that it represents a certain way of behaving or thinking in response to a particular kind of external, social stimulus in a given context. Here convention is *constructed* rather than *historical* because it is a specified group of people who 'invent' the convention and provides it with social warranty.

13 See Kirkham's (1992) outline of the correspondence theory of truth for a short discussion of the objection and some possible responses.

14 A note of clarification: in his 1990 paper quoted here, Davidson abandons the correspondence theory of truth for which he previously had argued so forcefully (e.g., in "True to the Facts" from 1969).

4   The coherence criterion of truth

What, then, is coherence? Intuitively, coherence is a matter of how well a body of beliefs "hangs together": how well its component beliefs fit together, agree or dovetail with each other, so as to produce an organized, tightly structured system of beliefs, rather than either a helter-skelter collection or a set of conflicting subsystems. It is reasonably clear that this "hanging together" depends on the various sorts of inferential, evidential, and explanatory relations which obtain among the various members of a system of beliefs, and especially on the more holistic and systematic of these.

Laurence BonJour, *The Structure of Empirical Knowledge*

4.1   Key components of the coherence theory

The coherence theory is one of the most influential epistemic frameworks in the modern history of philosophy (Bender 1989; Blanshard 1939; BonJour 1985; Bradley 1914; Davidson 1986; Lehrer 1990; Quine 1951; Rescher 1973; Walker 1989) and continues to influence developments on truth and epistemic justification (Hansson 2007; Poston 2014; Šešelja and Straßer 2014). Historically, the main rival theory is the correspondence theory of truth. Both theories agree that truth is a relational function of propositional content: propositions are true or false relative to their referential relation to X. What the theories disagree fundamentally about is what the alethic object of the referential relation is. We saw that the correspondence theory holds external objective facts to be the proper alethic referent. By contrast, coherentism shifts focus away from external reality and puts other propositions at the core. Accordingly, a propositional claim that P_1 is true insofar as it coheres with other propositional claims, $P_2–P_n$, in a specified set, S, of propositions. Propositions form a web or network of beliefs, and it is the interconnections in this holistic epistemic circuit that determine the truthfulness of any given proposition. Joachim (1939, 66) puts the holistic dimension of coherentism this way:

> To 'conceive' means for us to think out clearly and logically, to hold many elements together in a connexion necessitated by their several

contents. And to be 'conceivable' means to be a 'significant whole', or a whole possessed of meaning and thought. A 'significant whole' is such that all its constituent elements reciprocally involve one another, or reciprocally determine one another's being as contributory features in a single concrete meaning. The elements thus cohering constitute a whole which may be said to control the reciprocal adjustment of its elements, as an end controls its constituent means.

The correspondence theory frames alethic reference as a one-directional relation between a proposition and some external states of affairs. The coherence theory, by contrast, operationalizes alethic relations as pervasive multidirectional epistemic connections such that any belief is being justified by its relation to other beliefs, whilst at the same time contributing actively to the justification of the total set of beliefs (Haack 1993). Mutual justification is key: the degree to which propositions fit together determines what we are justified in believing and what we ultimately know. Quine (1951, 39), in his seminal paper *Two Dogmas of Empiricism*, expresses this insight as follows:

> [S]cience is like a field of force whose boundary conditions are experience. A conflict with experience at the periphery occasions readjustments in the interior of the field. Truth values have to be redistributed over some of our statements. Re-evaluation of some statements entails re-evaluation of others, because of their logical interconnections.

Another defining difference between coherence and correspondence theories is thereby shaping up: correspondence theories are linear and always progress from a fundamental, empirically grounded belief or observation, which transmits alethic properties to subordinate beliefs. Contrary to this, the coherence theory is circular and non-empirical: no type of belief (empirical, logical, intuitionistic) enjoys epistemic primacy, and all beliefs contribute to the epistemic status of the entire network of beliefs.[1]

Any attempt to flesh out the coherence theory in greater detail will have to take into account two core questions. First, what is meant by coherence? Over time, epistemologists have converged on the following candidates: inferential connectivity (BonJour 1985; Haack 1993; Rescher 1973)[2], explanatory coherence (Read and Marcus-Newhall 1993; Sloman 1994; Thagard 1989, 2000, 2012) and probability (Douven and Meijs 2007; Koscholke 2015; Moretti and Akiba 2007; Schippers 2014). What exactly is to be meant by each of the determinants is still subject to debate, but there is consensus that a serious coherence theory must provide a reasonable and productive definition of one or more of these alethic desiderata. Explanatory power and probability are mainstream epistemic constraints of most contemporary theories of truth. Inferential connectivity is the unique alethic characteristic of coherentism, and it plays the predominant role in establishing truth in marketing. I will therefore concentrate the discussion of coherence on that criterion. Rescher (1973, 173) nicely captures the foundational character of inferential connectivity in this quotation:

> The essential distinctiveness of the coherence theory lies in its utilization of the following precepts: (I) the truth of a proposition is to be determined in terms of its relationship to other propositions in its logico-epistemic environment. And consequently, (II) the true propositions form one tightly knit unit, a set each element of which stands in logical interlinkage with others so that the whole forms a comprehensively connected and unified network.

Second, it is necessary to clarify the constitution of the specified set of beliefs. As Young (2015) points out, there is agreement that the specified set comprises propositional entities (e.g., beliefs, assumptions) that a group of epistemic agents believe or hold to be true, but there is considerable disagreement over who counts as relevant epistemic agents. Young (1995) argues that the specified set comprises the largest set of consistent propositional entities believed by actual epistemic agents at a given point in time. Putnam (1981) offers a counterfactual interpretation and defines the specified set as the largest set of consistent propositional entities, which would be believed or held to be true by rational agents with a cognitive outlook like human beings at some limit of investigation. Putnam's interpretation strikes a strong chord with Peirce's conceptualization of truth as 'the end of inquiry'. At first glance, our case of truth in marketing seems to offer an intuitive solution: the specified set is the total set of propositional entities conveyed by the brand via its marketing communications. However, as will become apparent during the subsequent analysis, this interpretation is flawed.

Figure 4.1 outlines the core idea of the classical coherence theory of truth.

4.2 Symbolic value and symbolic claims

In what follows, I will develop a coherence criterion that accounts for the truth of symbolic marketing claims. As previously defined, symbolic marketing claims promise to associate the targeted consumer with symbolic values (such as masculinity, elegance, confidence and attractiveness), which are deemed socially desirable within a given reference group. The process for determining the truth or falsity of symbolic claims is much more challenging than was the case for functional claims. The truth of functional claims can be settled by empirical tests and verification, but this is not the case for symbolic claims. There are no objects in the external world to

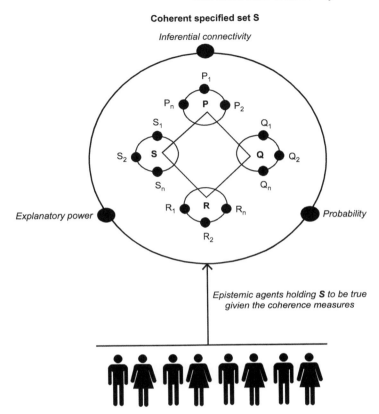

Figure 4.1 Conceptual model of the coherence theory of truth, comprising a coherent specified set, S, of propositional entities, (P, Q ...) and subsets thereof (P_1-P_n, Q_1-Q_n ...) that are mutually justifying in terms of three coherence measures (inferential connectivity, explanatory power and probability).

which symbolic claims refer: they correlate the use of products with socially desirable values, but neither the product nor the consumptional practice can work as referential object. The reason is that whereas functional claims are descriptive, symbolic claims are expressive or emotive. As the following analysis will demonstrate, symbolic value is closely linked with consumer associations, which means that the truth-making features are, in part, to be found in the mind of the consumer rather than in the external world.

In order to evaluate the veracity of symbolic claims, it will prove useful to provide a more detailed understanding of what symbolic values actually are. The next section uses Bourdieu's notion of symbolic capital as a platform to progress a marketing-specific definition of symbolic value.

The relevance of Bourdieu's concept of symbolic capital

Bourdieu's fundamental project is to understand the social preconditions of structural inequality. The core constituents of his complex theory are the notions of field, habitus and capital. In this context, it is his understanding of capital that is of interest. Bourdieu (1984, 1998) distinguishes between at least four different forms of human capital: economic, social, cultural and symbolic. The idea is that the courses of action open to an agent at any specific point of time within a social context (field) is determined by her distinctive mix of capital. Economic capital expresses one's ability to engage in monetary exchanges. Social capital is the total aggregate of individual resources linked to social recognition and social networks. Cultural capital comprises the individual's beliefs, assumptions and behavioural patterns as shaped by domestic and formal institutional education. Symbolic capital works as a kind of filtering device through which the other capital forms are transubstantiated. Symbolic capital is the value that other social agents attach to an individual agent, given the relevant reference groups' appreciation of the perceived set of capital possessed by the agent.

For example, although economic capital is the most fluid form of capital that can most easily be transubstantiated into cultural or social capital, the distinct symbolic capital attributed by other social agents may significantly influence the social worth or recognition of economic capital. This is precisely the case with the distinction between 'new money' and 'old money' where those in possession of 'new money' are financially rich but culturally poor compared to the class of people in possession of 'old money'. Another example of the power of symbolic capital is art: a work of modern art may consist in a heap of rubbish, but the artistic intention and the presentation of the artefact in an established gallery – the symbolic value attached to it – transubstantiate the objectively worthless material into a social object of potentially substantial economic, social and cultural value. This is why symbolic capital matters.

It is no surprise that the notion of symbolic capital is *not* equivalent to the concept of symbolic value in the theory of truth in marketing.[3] But there are important insights that elucidate the role of symbolic value in marketing as such, and I will now adapt the concept to the purpose of this exploration.

Symbolic value in marketing

From the point of view of epistemological psychology, symbolic capital is a conventional disposition to attribute associations to other people based on shared perceptions of their social standing. This shorthand definition comes very close to the influential conceptualisation of a brand as a set of associations (Keller 1993, 2001, 2008; Keller, Sternthal, and Tybout 2002).[4] The interest of marketers in associations is the assumption that a brand is an immaterial entity that only exists in the consumer mind-set. Of course, a brand may also be characterized as a trademark, logo, colour scheme, legal entity and so on, but all these aspects have value only insofar as consumers recognize them as such. To stay with Bourdieu, the brand's different capital forms (i.e., the core brand building blocks) have value only insofar as consumers recognize them as valuable by attaching favourable associations to the brand. Consumers' brand associations thereby adopt the crucial functional role of attaching symbolic value to the brand.

Accordingly, I define symbolic value as follows: a brand's symbolic value consists in the total set of targeted consumers' dispositional attribution of meaningful associations to the brand in response to relevant streams of marketing communication within a given time horizon.

This understanding of symbolic value has a very important implication for the development of a marketing-specific coherence criterion. The opening section of this chapter mentioned the problems associated with identifying the specified set of propositional entities with which (symbolic) claims must cohere. We are now in a position to see the shortcomings of the intuitively appealing solution of putting down the specified set as the totality of coherent propositional content conveyed by the brand within a specified time horizon. The challenge is that symbolic value, and thereby symbolic meaning, is partly driven by consumer perceptions and associations, which may be at odds with the brand universe as constructed via marketing efforts. As symbolic value and therefore also symbolic meaning are partly determined by consumer associations, symbolic claims have to cohere with, say, the largest set of shared consumer associations in the target group. But there is no guarantee that this will be the case. Thus, a symbolic claim may cohere with the marketing-constructed brand universe, whereas consumer interpretations of that claim may run counter to the propositional content of the brand universe.

4.3 Symbolic truth as internal and external coherence

An important distinction is now emerging: there are two different dimensions of coherence – internal and external – which are relevant to the truth evaluation of symbolic claims. Internally, symbolic claims convey a carefully designed message, which the brand hopes will instil a certain emotional reaction in the consumer and establish a favourable, associative connection to the brand. On this internal dimension, then, symbolic claims are true to the extent that they cohere with the official brand universe as constructed through marketing efforts. Symbolic truth becomes a function of coherence by design. The specified set with which symbolic claims must cohere is an aggregate of propositional content previously communicated by the brand.

Externally, consumers embedded in consumption contexts interpret symbolic marketing claims. These contexts are characterized by consumer attributions of social values to other consumers (peers) based on the actual use of brands as narrative material to construct and express self-identity and personal values (Annamma and Li 2012; Arnould and Thompson 2005; Schembri, Merrilees, and Kristiansen 2010). On this external dimension, then, symbolic claims are true relative to consumer propensity to attribute the emotional or expressive meaning of the symbolic claims to other consumers and, thereby, to the brand. Symbolic truth becomes a matter of coherence with the propositional content embedded in consumers' associative mode of reaction. In this case, the specified set is made up of shared consumer associations.

Accordingly, there are two specified sets of propositional entities: an internal set, S^I, that expresses coherence by design, and an external set, S^E, that expresses coherence by associative response. I define the truth of symbolic claims for each set as follows:

Internal coherence[5]

Let S^I be the total set of propositional content created by marketers within a given period of time, t_1–t_n, deemed relevant to the establishment of the coherence of a symbolic claim. Then, a symbolic marketing claim, P, is true at t insofar as P coheres with the key propositional content in S^I.

External coherence

Let S^E be the maximally coherent set of shared associations attached to a brand by the target consumers, C, within a given period of time, t_1–t_n, deemed relevant to the establishment of the coherence of a symbolic claim. Then, a symbolic marketing claim, P, is true at t insofar as P coheres with S^E such that C is likely to associate the individual brand user with the symbolic value conveyed by P.

Although both definitions are metaphysically fundamental to the establishment of symbolic truth in marketing, this exploration will focus exclusively on internal coherence. The principal reason is that external coherence is to a large extent out of the marketers' control. It is beyond doubt that brands invest vast amounts of money in marketing only because they hope – and believe – that marketing is effective in shaping consumer perceptions of brands, services and products. Yet, the power of marketing communications is impeded by at least two factors. First, media-literate consumers are aware of profit maximisation underpinning corporate activity, and this translates into a generally critical attitude to marketing communications (Austin et al. 2006; Buckingham 2006). This means that consumers' brand associations are not just simple causal, associative responses to marketing communications, but are usually more complex, interpretive reactions. Second, Anker et al. (2015) has recently demonstrated how consumers are actively engaged in creating, manipulating and changing the meaning of brands. For example, they discuss how one consumer group's adoption of the Burberry brand tarnished its image and ultimately made the brand undergo a radical repositioning to alienate the unwanted consumers and weaken their negative influence on consumer perceptions of the brand.[6]

The alethic link between symbolic claims and coherence

The truth of symbolic claims has now been defined as a dual function of (a) coherence with target consumers' shared brand associations (external coherence), and (b) coherence with key propositional content in the brand universe (internal coherence). But the underlying question of why coherence should be a relevant alethic criterion has not been addressed. What is it about symbolic claims that motivates the application of coherentism as a test of truthfulness? I will now establish a direct alethic link between internal coherence and symbolic claims.

It is perhaps trivial to observe that the promise of symbolic claims to transfer desirable social values onto the brand user can materialize only if the reference group perceives of the brand as conveying the relevant values. What is *not* trivial is how this collective set of associations is constituted. This is where internal coherence comes into the mix.

Roughly, internal coherence provides either positive or negative alethic support to symbolic claims. Positive alethic support occurs when the symbolic claim coheres with key propositional entities in the brand universe, such as established brand values. Contrariwise, negative support is the case when a brand makes symbolic claims that do not resonate with the established brand universe. Based on positive alethic support, it is possible to assign probabilities of brand users being associated with the desirable values promised by the symbolic claim: the stronger the degree of fit between the symbolic claim and the brand universe, the higher the likelihood that consumers will associate the brand with the value and, subsequently, attribute the symbolic value to individual brand users. Internal coherence is thereby a facilitator of external coherence and, ultimately, symbolic truth.

An example will prove useful. Skoda, the carmaker, has established itself as a strong consumer brand since VW acquired the company almost 25 years ago. Today, the car brand stands for reliability, affordability and family orientation. These core brand values have recently been further substantiated by Skoda winning the prestigious Best Family Car title in the 2014 *What Car? Awards*. Like most brands, however, even Skoda sometimes makes a blunder. One example is two separate ad campaigns – one in Ireland, the other in Germany – that have been accused of sexism (Withnall 2013). In Ireland, Skoda ran a newspaper ad featuring a groom pondering whether to "Give her [the car/the bride] back to daddy", "Trade her in for her younger sister" or "Keep her". The ad caused a consumer backlash on social media. In Germany, a Skoda ad featuring two breasts in a tight top with one nipple erected was used to launch a new Skoda Octavia.

In this context, the normative dimension of sexism in advertising is not the concern. The example is interesting because it provides a situation where a brand is communicating symbolic claims that are semantically isolated in the sense that they employ a theme, which is not consistent with the brand's advertising history and runs counter to the established brand values. The consumer reactions provide an opportunity to assess the normative dimension of the campaign. By contrast, the lack of coherence with the brand universe offers an opportunity to assess the veracity of the sexualized symbolic claims: the claims are untrue because they receive negative alethic support from the brand universe and, thereby, have a very low probability of influencing target consumers to associate brand users with the sexualized properties conveyed by the claims.

Figure 4.2 provides an overview of the connection between symbolic truth and coherence.

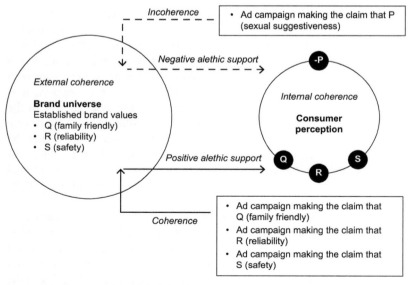

Figure 4.2 Conceptual model of the alethic link between symbolic claims and internal/external coherence.

4.4   The nature of coherence: inferential connectivity

Having defined truth of symbolic claims in terms of internal and external coherence and answered the question as to why coherence is a relevant alethic measure, it is now time to unpack what should be meant by coherence. What is it for a propositional entity (such as a marketing claim) to cohere with another propositional entity or sets thereof?

The main idea of coherentism is to construe epistemic justification and truth as a matter of mutual support between propositional entities. It follows from that baseline assumption that if a coherent set of propositions, S, entails or implies another proposition, P, or a subset of propositions, *s*, then the inferred propositional entities, P and *s*, must also be coherent members of S. Accordingly, there is strong agreement that one predominant aspect of coherence is inferential connectivity. BonJour (1985, 98), one of the key contributors to the modern development of coherentism, observes that:

> [t]he coherence of a system of beliefs is increased by the presence of inferential connections between its component beliefs and increased in proportion to the number and strength of such connections.

But it has proved remarkably difficult to arrive at a shared understanding of what type of inferential connectivity is conducive to epistemic coherence. Deductive entailment is the most obvious candidate because this type of inference guarantees truth: if one of the established rules of inference is followed in a deductive inference from a set of true premises, then the truth of the conclusion is necessarily true. Rescher's interpretation of the coherence theory is an effort to formulate a formal theory of coherence, predominantly founded on deductive inferential connectivity.

But inferential connectivity is not exhausted by formal logic, and Schippers (2014, 3822) notes that "limiting coherence-boosting inferential connections to deductive entailment would deprive the concept of coherence of epistemological applicability". In marketing, the principal interest in inferential connectivity is the ability to assess whether a certain narrative influences, or would be likely to influence, the target audience to develop certain beliefs, or convince them of important beliefs being true or false. The theory of truth in marketing should therefore employ a non-formal type of inferential connectivity.

To this end, the distinction between logical entailment and conversational implicature (Grice 1989) is highly relevant and productive. Logical entailment occurs whenever the truth of one claim follows logically from the truth of another claim. In its simplest form, logical entailment takes the following form: 'All Danes are Vikings. Thomas is a Dane. Thomas is a Viking.' The conclusion 'Thomas is a Viking' follows with necessity from the two preceding premises. Logical entailment is a formal inferential connection between propositions that is entirely independent from the actual content and meaning of the propositions as well as their actual truth status. Even if it should turn out to be false that all Danes are Vikings, the actual falsity of the premise does not influence the truth of the conclusion.

By contrast, conversational implicature is characterized by inferential connections that are justified through the actual content of a given narrative and the context in which it is communicated (Atlas 2005; Grice 1989; Levinson 2000). For example, a parent's utterance, 'Your socks are lying on the floor', aimed at a lazy teenager might not convey a factual, empirical observation, but rather communicate an order to put the socks in the laundry bin. In this case, the intended meaning of the claim is communicated via an implicit inferential structure that is activated and authorized by an understanding of the context of communication.

Grice (1989) coined the term 'conversational implicature' and was the first philosopher of language to systematically explore this universal feature of ordinary, informal language.[7] Grice's (1989, 26) theory of meaning is based on the following cooperative principle:

> Make your conversational contribution such as is required, at the stage at which it occurs, by the accepted purpose or direction of the talk exchange in which you are engaged. One might label this the Cooperative Principle.

The cooperative principle is associated with four conversational maxims related to quality, quantity, relation and manner. Here, quality and quantity are of principal interest. The maxim of quality concerns claim–evidence relations in conversational contexts and states that a speaker should always aim at making her contribution true. The maxim of quantity holds that any conversational contribution should be as informative as required and sufficient.

Conversational implicature plays a crucial role in the theory of truth in marketing: the subsequent analysis demonstrates that the concept can account for different types of misleading advertising with respect to both symbolic and functional claims. The conversational implicature of an ad establishes what is true in the world of the ad: there is strong supporting evidence that if the narrative context of an ad – be it an imaginative or factual story – implies that something, X, is the case, then X should be assumed to be the case in the ad, regardless of whether X is true or false in the external world.

Here is an example of how conversational implicature is used in practise to establish truth in marketing. In May 2015, the ASA (2015b) ruled that a double-page Vogue ad for the Prada-owned clothing brand, Miu Miu, displayed a sexualized child. In its response to ASA's interpretation, Prada emphasized that the model featured in the ad was a 22-year-old actress. Interestingly, this reference to the actual state of affairs in the external world did not change the view of the advertising adjudicator, which maintained that the ad sexualized a child and, therefore, was offensive. The ASA's full assessment of the ad is as follows:

> The ASA noted that the model had a youthful appearance, was wearing very minimal make up and clothes that appeared to be slightly too large. We considered those elements contributed to the impression that she was younger than 16 years of age. She was posed reclining on a bed, looking up directly to the camera through a partially opened door, which gave her an air of vulnerability and the image a voyeuristic feel. We considered that the crumpled sheets and her partially opened mouth also enhanced the impression that her pose was sexually suggestive. We considered that her youthful appearance, in conjunction with the setting and pose, could give the impression that the ad presented a child in a sexualised way. Therefore, we concluded that the ad was irresponsible and was likely to cause serious offence.

This example perfectly demonstrates how conversational implicature may determine the truth or falsity of symbolic claims. The ASA's judgement that the ad sexualizes a child is entirely based on an interpretation of what associations the narrative of the ad *implies*. The adjudicator's disregard for external facts is obvious and explicit: the fact that the model is *not* a child does not affect what the ad is *truly about* in terms of what the ad *implies* or *suggests*. Here, then, truth is established as a clear-cut application of conversational implicature. The broader link to the previous definition of truth as internal coherence is also very clear: the conversational implicature (i.e., that the ad sexualizes a child) is founded on internal coherence in the sense that what the ad is *truly* about is a function of what the various different communication vehicles employed in the ad (the clothing, the make-up, the camera angle) imply when viewed as a *coherent structure*.

A number of ASA rulings are structurally identical to this case, suggesting that to rely on the imaginative elements of the ad-universe to establish actual claim–evidence relations is a commonplace practice. In particular, there are a number of ASA rulings on inappropriate sexualization of women and sexualization of children where the inferential scheme used to establish the claim–evidence relations is identical to the case just discussed. See, for example, two recent ASA (2012b, 2015a) rulings on American Apparel. But truth by conversational implicature is not restricted to any particular theme or type of advertising. Conversational implicature can also determine the truthfulness of functional claims.

This is demonstrated by ASA's (2014b) ruling on a Disney ad, where the adjudicator employed the same inferential pattern to establish what the ad truly said. The ad was marketing Disney's Bibbidi Bobbidi Boutique, which among other things allows children the opportunity to dress up in princess or knight costumes, having their hair styled, and so on. The ad featured a young girl transported by imagination into a princess world, but did not show any boys in knight costumes. However, the advertised minimum price of £50 was for the 'knight experience'. ASA ruled that the ad misleadingly implied that the minimum price of the 'princess experience' was £50. Again, what the ad truly says is established through conversational implicature, which in turn is established through a thorough interpretation of the various semantic elements embedded in the ad's narrative universe.

The cases just discussed relate to the general concept of conversational implicature. However, at least some of the specific maxims associated with Grice's cooperative principle are also relevant to establishing truth in marketing. As mentioned, the maxim of quantity requires communicators to provide sufficient amounts of information relative to the overall purpose of the communication. In marketing, violating the Gricean principle of quantity may lead to a breakdown of inferential connectivity, with potentially serious implications. The following example demonstrates how the conversational implicature of an ad failed to establish crucial facts about the product and, thereby, lied to the consumer. In January 2015, ASA (2015c) ruled that an ad for Unibet, a gambling website, was misleading. The ad said:

> Will Man City beat Liverpool? Join Unibet for a £20 Risk Free Bet on today's game! MANCHESTER CITY V LIVERPOOL £20 RISK FREE BET. ... Open an account today and we will cover the risk of your first bet up to £20.

ASA found the ad to be misleading because the conversational context did not suggest that it would be necessary to place further bets and that the offer would be "subject to significant limitations and exclusions". Put differently, the ad lied to consumers because the true nature of the advertised product did not follow from the conversational implicature. The ad violated Grice's quantity maxim and thereby led to false conversational implicature.

4.5   Objections

The coherence theory is confronted with a number of fundamental challenges. First, I will address the plurality objection, which is a classical problem that has been discussed during the lifespan of the theory. Without a solution to this problem, coherence theory is inconsistent. Second, I will address a recent innovation in the correspondence theory, which challenges the relevance of coherence as a criterion of truth in marketing.

The plurality objection

One of the most challenging objections is the possibility of multiple, maximally coherent specified sets, which are mutually incoherent and each of which one has good reason to believe.

According to coherentism, a proposition P is true insofar as P belongs to a specified set of coherent propositions, S. Coherentism thus defines truth in terms of some kind of mutual alethic transfer between propositions without any firm grounding in external, empirical facts. This gives rise to the following problem: at any point in time, t, it is possible for two specified sets of propositions, S_1 and S_2, to be equally coherent but mutually incompatible. For example, it may be possible that P is true in S_1, but false in S_2 at t.[8] (See Figure 4.3.) This is a counterintuitive – and incoherent – consequence of the theory, demonstrating a fundamental flaw in all coherence theories of truth and epistemic justification.[9]

This conclusion has obvious real-world relevance. Two systems of belief, say a religious and atheistic system, may be internally coherent but mutually incompatible because they comprise one or more subsets of beliefs that are inconsistent. The objection applies to marketing as well. Dove's *Campaign for Real Beauty* is one of the most successful marketing campaigns of recent time. The aim of the campaign is to fight dysfunctional stereotypes of female beauty and introduce alternative, inclusive ideals of beauty that can form the base of increased self-esteem among women and young girls. One part of the campaign is a series of viral videos that directly criticize the use of extremely thin young women portrayed as sexual objects. Perhaps the most striking example is the video *Onslaught* that effectively demonstrates how aggressive advertising has sexualized the public space. The video reminds the audience to "Talk to your children before the beauty industry does". The problem of incoherence and inconsistency appears because Dove is owned by Unilever which also owns Lynx. Lynx is a male body care brand whose advertising style is driven by the kind of female stereotypes that Dove decries. Lynx has been subject to a number

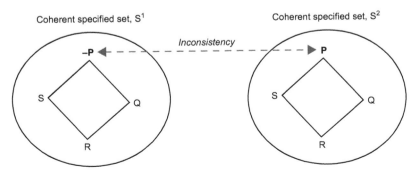

Figure 4.3 The plurality objection to coherentism.

of complaints for sexually offensive advertising. In one adjudication from 2011, the ASA (2011b) states:

> We considered that, alongside the strap line 'the cleaner you are the dirtier you get', the call to action at the bottom of the poster 'visit facebook.com/lynxeffect and get dirty this summer', was clearly intended to imply that using the advertised product would lead to more uninhibited sexual behaviour. We therefore considered that the poster would be seen to make a link between purchasing the product and sex with women and in so doing would be seen to objectify women.

Both Dove and Lynx belong to the same overarching brand domain comprised by Unilever's brand portfolio. Understanding each of the product brands as distinct brand universes that belong to the same meta-brand universe (brand portfolio), we then have two specified sets containing mutually inconsistent propositional content. This places us in a scenario that is seemingly relevantly identical to the one that gave rise to the standard objection. However, I will argue that the objection is only of concern to pure epistemology. In applied epistemology, the problem becomes an operational concern that can be addressed by rational determination of the scope of inquiry.

In applied epistemology, a key constituent of a specified set is the scope of the domain of inquiry. And that scope can only be determined by the epistemic agents inquiring the domain. For our purposes, a set of beliefs, s, is a specified set, S, in a given domain of inquiry, D, insofar as the epistemic agents responsible for the inquiry have agreed that s is identical to S in D. This may seem like a circumvention, but is far from it. It is a practical consequence of the application of coherentism in practical domains of inquiry. This is evidenced by the actual application of the coherence criterion by marketing regulators and adjudicators such as the ASA.

When marketing regulators receive a complaint, they have to establish whether the claim should be judged in isolation or in a broader context. For example, it needs to be determined if the complaint is one that addresses the relation between a marketing claim and a specific product (such as a potentially misleading nutrition claim) or whether the complaint addresses aspects of the wider brand context (such as a claim about brand heritage). The specified set will be determined by this consideration. For example, the ASA's (2011a) handling of a complaint over a Nutella TV ad clearly demonstrates how the scope – and thereby the specified set – is determined by the aim of inquiry. Between November 2010 and February 2011, the ASA received 31 complaints over the TV ad, which they describe as follows:

> It showed various people, including children, waking up and going about their morning routines; they prepared toast with Nutella and left their homes dressed for work or school. It included a voice-over that

stated "Each 15 gram portion contains two whole hazelnuts, some skimmed milk and cocoa. ... Wake up to Nutella". Text on screen stated "wake up to Nutella".

The ASA received two different complaints. The first held that the ad was misleading because "it did not make clear that Nutella also contained a high proportion of sugar and fat". The second contended that the ad was "likely to encourage poor nutritional habits or an unhealthy lifestyle, especially in children". The ASA decided not to uphold any of the complaints.

The full adjudication demonstrates how the scope – in terms of the domain of relevant marketing content – is set differently for the two complaints. Regarding the first complaint, the ASA analyzed the relationship between what was actually said about the product during the ad and the content of the product. The assessment of the second complaint, by contrast, broadened the scope considerably and assessed the societal concern that people who skip breakfast are more likely to have less nutritious diets than those who eat breakfast. The ASA concluded that the ad encouraged children to eat breakfast without encouraging "poor nutritional habits or an unhealthy lifestyle in children".

The ruling shows how the specified set of relevant propositional content is determined by the nature of the inquiry: in the first situation, the specified set is the actual TV campaign; in the second situation the specified set includes a broader public health narrative.

Let us reconnect to the example with Dove and Lynx to see why this observation tackles the plurality objection. The reason we end up having two inconsistent specified sets is that we extend the scope such that two distinct and mutually incompatible brand universes come to belong to the same overarching brand universe (i.e., the same corporate brand portfolio). The problem can thereby be diagnosed as an instance of over-stretching the scope beyond what is of epistemic importance to the aim of inquiry. The objection is no longer systemic and insurmountable but operational and manageable because it is reduced to a function of determining the scope against the aim of inquiry.

There may be some dissatisfaction with this solution: some may find solving the problem by means of manipulating the scope of one's theory to be artificial and unwarranted. After all, the criticism of the apparent hypocrisy of Unilever in terms of sustaining two clashing brand universes (Dove/Lynx) shows that consumers care about the conduct of corporate brands.[10] Indeed, in this particular case, consumers make normative judgements regarding the corporate brand, which resonate across the distinct brand universes that belong to the same parent brand. Consumers do not distinguish sharply between product and corporate brands, so why should we?

My view is that it is warranted to make the operational assumption that truth investigations should, under normal circumstances, be carried out at the product/service brand level insofar as the alethic concern being addressed has to do with a specific product/service brand. The scope of the theory is determined by the aim of inquiry. The aim of inquiry, in turn, is set in response to the nature of the communications that are under investigation. Thus, if a truth assessment concerns brand claims that refer to entities within the same brand universe (i.e., reference to the brand's products and services), then the aim of the truth investigation will naturally be set against this and the scope of the theory will be adjusted accordingly. This renders irrelevant any discomfort with potential clashes between distinct brands that belong to the same parent brand.

Correspondence, response-dependency and symbolic claims

This chapter argues that the coherence theory of truth should be employed to account for the truth of symbolic claims. However, recent developments surrounding the correspondence theory of truth challenge this assumption. López de Sa (2010) has extended correspondence to accommodate response-dependent properties, a tweak that substantially increases the scope and explanatory power of the theory. Some may argue that fitting the correspondence theory with a response-dependent device enables it to explain symbolic truths, thus rendering coherence irrelevant. The argument could go like this.

Properties like 'funny', 'sexy' and 'tasty' are response-dependent in the sense that they only materialize under conditions where people exhibit a certain type of response.[11] Thus, it may hold true that a film is funny, but only under normal circumstances and for a designated set of people. For example, a given target group has a certain dispositional make-up resulting in their finding a certain TV-series, say *Family Guy*, to be funny under normal circumstances (e.g., when lying on the couch Friday night with a cold beer in hand). Symbolic claims in marketing have a striking resemblance to response-dependent properties: they promise to associate the user with desirable values (such as sexual attraction), which are perfectly analysable in terms of response-dependency and, therefore, fall within the explicative scope of the updated correspondence theory.

But discarding the coherence theory of truth would still be a serious drawback. I introduced the distinction between internal and external coherence to account for two important alethic dimensions of symbolic claims, and the response-dependent device is only applicable to external coherence. The current state of play therefore is that coherence is a necessary alethic criterion. But given the dramatically increased scope of the correspondence theory to range over both factual and symbolic domains, future research should explore whether the theory could be further augmented, with a view to establish whether a monistic theory of truth in marketing would be feasible.

4.6 Conclusion

Symbolic claims promise to associate the brand user with desirable social values. This chapter argued that the coherence theory of truth accounts for two different dimensions of symbolic truth in marketing. First, insofar as symbolic truth is conditioned on associative relations between the brand and the brand user, the user's peer reference group is fundamental to the materialization of symbolic claims. Thus, symbolic claims are true in terms of *external coherence* when consumers in relevant target groups are likely to associate the brand users with the social values conveyed by the symbolic claim. As consumers have significant capability to influence the perceived meaning of brands, external coherence is only partially under the control of the brand. Since the focus of this exploration lies predominantly on claim–evidence relations in the intersection between brand and consumer agency, external coherence was not investigated in any detail.

Second, symbolic truth is alethically connected to the epistemic status of the brand universe. Consumers' propensity to attribute the symbolic values conveyed by a brand to the brand users is shaped by the semantic power of the brand universe. A brand universe inhabited by meaningful propositional content is therefore a key indicator of symbolic truth. Accordingly, a symbolic claim is true in terms of *internal coherence* to the extent that the claim coheres with the key propositional content in the brand universe, as constructed by the brand. There are differing views on the nature of coherence, but for the purposes of this study inferential connectivity – the unique differentiator of coherentism – should be the main epistemic criterion to determine the (internal) alethic status of symbolic claims. Relying on

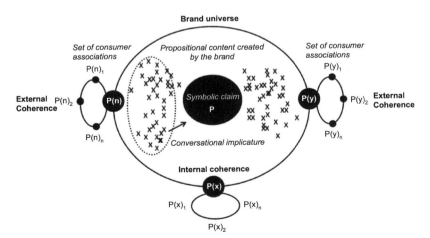

Figure 4.4 Conceptual model of the truth of symbolic claims in marketing.

Grice's seminal work on informal, narrative inference, I discussed how the conversational implicatures embedded in the narrative structure of brand universes imply certain propositional content. A symbolic claim is true insofar as the conversational implicature of the brand universe implies the symbolic value conveyed by the claim. Figure 4.4 summarizes the definition of symbolic truth in marketing.

Notes

1   Haack (1993) has developed a crossover theory of truth that merges the driving intuitions of the correspondence and coherence theories of truth. The theory, dubbed 'foundherentism', takes inferential connectivity (coherentism) to be the key epistemic characteristic of truth but holds that not all propositions are equal in terms of epistemic importance: some empirically founded beliefs play a heavier role in justifying our beliefs and are therefore more foundational than others (empiricism/foundationalism/correspondence).

2   Early coherence theories stressed consistency as the key epistemic determinant (Young 2015). However, consistency is by no means unique to coherentism; rather, it is a fundamental baseline requirement for any theory of truth. Moreover, consistency is embedded as a subcriterion of inferential connectivity: one set of propositions, P_1–P_3, can only entail another proposition, P_4, if the latter is consistent with the former.

3   Historically, there is a strong link between the notion of symbolic value and consumption practices. Veblen's (1899) seminal book, *The Theory of the Leisure Class*, provided the first systematic exploration of conspicuous consumption conceptualized as a form of symbolic consumption. With Veblen and Bourdieu, Baudrillard (1981, 1998) makes the case that economic transactions involve the production of differential sign value; that is, consumption is a means of constructing and expressing symbolic value.

4   According to Keller (1993, 2001), one of the leading authors on brand equity, consumer associations are a fundamental brand building block. For example, brand image is interpreted as a function of strength, favourability and uniqueness of brand associations.

5   Chapter 5 argues that brand heritage (i.e., the entire history of a brand) functions as an epistemic warrant that enables consumers to judge whether a brand's alethic facilitation of behavioural claims is trustworthy. In terms of internal coherence, the truth of symbolic claims will, in the most extreme cases, depend on consistency with all propositional content embedded in the entire brand heritage.

6   This case is colloquially known as Burberry's 'Chav challenge' (Bothwell 2005; Economist 2011; Hayward and Yar 2006).

7   Grandy and Warner (2014) provide a good overview of Grice's philosophy of language and explains the central role of conversational implicature in his theory of meaning.

8   This standard objection to coherentism goes under different names such as the plurality objection (Dancy 1998), the alternative systems objection (Poston 2014) and the specification objection (Young 2015). It is conceptually closely related to another challenge, often called the input objection (BonJour 1985; Poston 2014), as the root of both problems is the contentious relation

between the specified set of coherent propositional entities and the external empirical world.

9 Pioneering coherentists such as Bradley (1914) and Blanshard (1939) addressed the plurality objection. They argue that the objection is unsuccessful in refuting coherentism because there is one, and just one, specified set of coherent propositional content, namely, the network of beliefs and assumptions based on empirical experience. All competing specified sets would be non-empirical and, thereby, fail to account for our sense experience. Unfortunately, this defense of the coherence theory is not compelling because it violates the driving intuition of coherentism, that is, that propositional entities are justified through their epistemic connection to other propositional entities. Bradley and Blanshard foreshadow Haack's (1993) crossover theory 'foundherentism'.

10 Internet searches using key words like "Dove-Lynx controversy" or "Dove, Lynx, Unilever hypocrisy" show widespread consumer and media engagement in the discussion of the normative clash between the Dove and Lynx brands and the ethical implications this is taken to have for the parent brand, Unilever.

11 Johnston (1989) coined the term 'response-dependent concept'.

5   The instrumental criterion of truth

> Any idea upon which we can ride, so to speak; any idea that will carry us
> prosperously from any one part of our experience to any other part, linking
> things satisfactorily, working securely, simplifying, saving labor; it is true
> for just so much, true in so far forth, true *instrumentally.*
>
> William James, *Pragmatism*

5.1   The general idea

The instrumental criterion of truth applies to behavioural marketing claims
and propositions. I define behavioural claims as claims that state a functional
product benefit that can obtain only if the consumer adopts a specified course
of actions. In other words, the promised product benefit is not just conditional
on the consumption of the product but hinges on a broader set of actions that
the consumer must take. On this definition, the link between behavioural
claims and the American pragmatists' instrumental criterion of truth is obvious: a behavioural product claim that P is true only if the consumer, C, acts
on P in a specified way. This reflects the core idea of the pragmatic maxim.

An example will prove useful. Health branding is one of the most obvious areas of abundant behavioural claims. When, say, a food health brand
such as Kellogg's Special K makes the claim that its product range helps
consumers lead a healthy lifestyle, then the most obvious conclusion seems
to be that the health brand promise is either misleading or plain false – the
reason being that eating any number of bowls of cereals a day won't make
you healthy. Dietary health is not a simple function of consuming any particular food product, but a complex function of a balanced diet maintained
over time.

This conclusion, however, is based on interpreting the health brand
promise as a standard functional claim, which is delivered – made true –
by product-inherent properties and features. If, on the contrary, the health
brand promise is interpreted in instrumental terms as a claim the truth of
which depends on a broader set of actions, then the claim may be sensible
and truthful. A health brand claim such as 'Brand X promises to enhance or

maintain your health' is true insofar as the brand facilitates courses of action that will allow the consumer to lead a healthy lifestyle.

In this broader sense, Special K comes much closer to delivering on its health promise: the brand provides a number of tools designed to help consumers lead a healthy lifestyle such as personalized meal plans, online communities that provide support and advice, weight management programmes and exercise tips, all integrated in a mobile app. If the consumer engages with the brand at this broader level that reaches far and beyond consuming the core product, then it is very reasonable to expect that the consumer will maintain or improve his or her health status. The health brand promise is thus delivered via the consumer's adoption of certain behavioural patterns that are encouraged and facilitated by the brand. This is the core pragmatic idea of truth in action!

The general idea is that a behavioural marketing claim is true insofar as the brand communicating the claim facilitates courses of actions that, if adopted by the consumer, will make the claim true. I will now define this broad idea and discuss various aspects of the definition as well as the associated notion of epistemic justification.

Instrumental truth: generic definition
A behavioural marketing claim that P is true insofar as the brand facilitates a course of action, X, such that if the consumer, C, embarks on X, then as a consequence P will obtain at some point in the future.

The generic definition captures the core idea of instrumental truth in marketing, but it needs precision and clarification in terms of targeting and segmentation; alethic facilitation and responsibility; normativity; and epistemic justification.

5.2   Truth, segmentation and targeting

Behavioural claims have to take into account the determining characteristics of the consumer profile, the relevant segmentation variables and the target of the marketing communications.

A telling example is the mass marketing of sports drinks. A 2012 edition of the BBC TV programme *Panorama* (BBC 2012) titled *The Truth about Sports Products*, which relies on studies published in the *British Medical Journal* (Cohen 2012; Heneghan et al. 2012), documents how the mass marketing of the sports drink, Lucozade, fails to deliver on core claims. Lucozade, which is produced and marketed by GlaxoSmithKline, promises performance-enhancing benefits during physical exercise. The product claims are true on a narrow interpretation of the correspondence theory of truth: professional athletes, such as the brand's celebrity endorser, Mo

Farah, may gain performance-enhancing benefits from carbohydrate ingestion when consuming the drink during exercise.

However, the average consumer of the product is unlikely to gain any performance-related benefits. Heneghan et al. (2012) conclude that Lucozade only enhances sports performance at high intensity, prolonged over a period of more than 90 minutes. This means that the average and targeted consumer – recreational athletes and children – will not experience any of the promised performance-enhancing benefits.

On an instrumental, behavioural interpretation of Lucozade's claim to enhance performance, the conclusion is that the required pattern of consumption that will bring about the advertised product benefit is not accessible or relevant to the targeted, average consumer of the product. The product claims are therefore instrumentally untrue. The material conditions are alethically restricted such that the truth property can be brought about through consumer–brand interaction within a specified range of truth-making agents (target consumers) only. Any generic product claims that span classes of consumers are made false by the inability of the average consumer to bring about the necessary pattern of consumption on which the behavioural truth property (performance enhancement) depends. Truth, thereby, is a function of targeted facilitation of relevant courses of actions that will bring about the promised behavioural property, if a clearly defined set of alethic agents were to act accordingly. The definition of behavioural truth therefore needs to reflect the idea that the relevant course of action should be doable and reasonable relative to the targeted, average consumer.

In fairness to the brand dimension, it is important that the qualification is 'targeted, average consumer' and not simply 'average consumer'. The rationale is that the following scenario of unintended mass consumption is perfectly possible: assume that (a) a given product (say, a sports drink), X, is genuinely targeted at a niche segment, S (such as professional athletes) and the product benefits hold true for S; (b) in spite of the niche targeting, X becomes a popular product among average consumers (recreational athletes); and (c) the product benefits do not hold true for the average consumer. In such a scenario, it would be unfair to hold brand X responsible for the fact that the product benefits do not obtain for the average consumer. The brand is not engaged in untrue or misleading marketing because it was never the intention to reach a mass market and all marketing efforts are, ex hypothesi, proven to be directed at the niche consumer segment.

5.3　Alethic facilitation and ontological truth

The fundamental role of the brand in the generic definition of instrumental truth is behavioural-epistemic facilitation: the brand enables the behavioural truth-makers (consumers) to realize the alethic properties of the behavioural product claim. This is what I call 'alethic facilitation'.

There are two main modes of alethic facilitation: (1) direct alethic facilitation, which occurs when the alethic property is supposed to emerge in direct interaction between the brand and the consumer; and (2) indirect alethic facilitation, which occurs when the consumer realizes the alethic property without interacting directly with the brand, but the course of actions that lead to the realization of the property are suggested, recommended and authorized by the brand.

Here is an example of how a brand employs both types of alethic facilitation. Dove's (2015) influential *Campaign for Real Beauty*, launched in 2004 and still running, aims at improving the bases of girl's and women's self-esteem by promoting more inclusive ideals of beauty. The main vehicle to this end is extensive use of models of shapes, sizes and colours that would not normally find their way to the billboards and glossy lifestyle magazines. The campaign employs different forms of direct alethic facilitation – for example, an educational programme in which the brand works directly with the targeted consumers, providing participants with tools to manage and react against societal pressure to conform to certain norms of appearance. Indirect alethic facilitation takes place, for example, through establishing consumer-to-consumer online communities designed to enable peer groups to share advice and experiences, and through publishing videos and short films such as *Onslaught* and *Evolution* that encourage parents to talk to their children about the negative impact of media-created stereotypes on self-esteem. Two comprehensive studies, *The Real Truth about Beauty: A Global Report* (2004) and *The Real Truth about Beauty: Revisited (2011)* are the anchors of extensive PR efforts aimed at influencing consumers to change attitude and behavior with regard to female stereotyping.

Alethic facilitation entails a reciprocal notion of responsibility: the brand and the consumer are mutually responsible for the materialization of the behavioural property. This part of the theory of truth in marketing departs fundamentally from the classical pragmatic theory of truth. The mutual alethic responsibility is an indicator of the social dimension of truth, rather than truthfulness as it would be in standard pragmatism. Consumers are necessary instruments of alethic instantiation in that the truth facilitation enabled by the brand is nothing more than a promise – a potentiality – the realization of which depends on consumer agency. Consumers and brands thereby co-create the truth and are not simply engaged in mutual chains of truthfulness. Peirce, James and Dewey do indeed operate with a social condition of truth (consensus), but that condition is *epistemological* rather than *ontological*. And that is the difference: in our case, consumers and brands co-create the truth (associated with behavioural claims) by jointly realizing the behavioural truth property. It is a two-way responsibility where both the brand (the alethic facilitator) and the consumer (the truth-maker) have to interact directly or indirectly in order for the truth property to be realized. As such, their alethic interaction is *ontological*.

5.4   Alethic responsibility

Behavioural truth emerges through consumer–brand interactions. This raises the question of how the alethic responsibility is shared between the two. External agents (the brand, peers, celebrities) contribute to the epistemological condition of the individual consumer as sources of knowledge. In marketing, this social epistemological condition is closely connected to the notion of doxastic control (Nottelmann 2008). Consumers are often in a condition of no doxastic control in the sense that they form a belief about a product or service in response to, and because of, being subject to a stream of marketing efforts. The very purpose of marketing is to communicate below the radar of individual doxastic control in order to have maximum influence on the target's desires, preferences and beliefs. Consequently, the brand is by definition having – or attempting to gain – significant doxastic influence over its target consumers and, therefore, holds substantial epistemic responsibility for the resulting beliefs. Thus, if a brand, X, intentionally induces the belief that P in a targeted consumer, A, in order to influence A to adopt a certain course of action, then X is doxastically responsible for: (a) A believing that P and, therefore, (b) the justification of P.

Given that behavioural truth emerges as a result of acting successfully on a particular belief over time, and that brands are responsible for inducing beliefs in consumers, then it is tempting to hold the brand fully responsible for the facilitation and realization of instrumental truth.[1]

However, the consumer has an important alethic responsibility. As Anker et al. (2012) point out in their discussion of experiential brands that make behavioural brand promises, it is the responsibility of the consumer to approach the brand with a certain willingness to interact. In our case, the behavioural truth property is contingent on the following individual dispositional attribution: willingness to engage in brand-facilitated courses of action over a sustained period of time.

This dispositional attribution is a reasonable condition of consumer responsibility because the absence of doxastic control does not entail absence of behavioural control. There is no causal connection between being motivated to do X and actually doing X. This intention–behaviour gap has been documented as a general social psychological phenomenon (Sheeran 2002) and in practical contexts such as ethical consumption (Carrington, Neville, and Whitwell 2010) and health behavior (Rhodes and de Bruijn 2013; Rhodes and Dickau 2012). There are multiple explanations for the intention–behaviour gap. Akrasia (weakness of the will) certainly accounts for some instances and would be an example of lack of behavioural control. Yet, other explanations are open. When consumers do not act on a given motivation, it may be a deliberate, rational act of choosing between competing motivations (e.g., price sensitivity versus ethical concerns). In such cases, consumers demonstrate the ability to override certain desires or preferences in light of critical reflection of the overall context of consumption.

Consumers' behavioural control can therefore be extended to contexts where agents do not have doxastic control. Put differently, consumers have the power to decide to act or not to act on marketing-induced beliefs, preferences and desires. It is therefore reasonable to assume that although A's belief that P is induced via marketing and may generate a certain motivation to engage in x course of action, A is still likely to be in a state of behavioural control such that she is capable of accepting or declining to act on the marketing-induced motivation to do x.

Proportionality as normative, operational criterion

Conditioning pragmatic truth on consumer willingness to engage with courses of actions facilitated by the brand calls for a clear demarcation of the limits of consumer–brand responsibility. One can easily imagine a brand that makes product claims that are true under conditions so extreme that it cannot meaningfully be the consumer's responsibility to willingly engage in the corresponding courses of actions facilitated by the brand. Anker et al. (2012) discuss the example of a retailer that makes a pledge (behavioural claim) to help consumers reduce their carbon footprint by 50% in 2020, but facilitates this through unreasonably demanding courses of actions. These actions would, for example, require consumers to go off grid and produce their own electricity, grow all their own vegetables, and only buy second-hand clothing.

The requirement of interaction necessitated by the nature of instrumental truth therefore needs to be qualified in terms of a criterion of proportionality. Alexy (2002, 2003), one of the most influential contributors to the development of the principle of proportionality, has provided a tripartite definition of proportionality in law, which has impacted international legal frameworks (Sweet and Matthews 2008). The definition constructs proportionality as a meta-constitutional rule (Sweet and Matthews 2008) designed to resolve hard cases of conflict between competing legal principles. Though related, our purpose is different: what is needed in this inquiry is an operational criterion that can guide the facilitation of courses of actions in contexts of consumption. Apart from building on Alexy's understanding of necessity as a subprinciple of proportionality, I shall therefore introduce a notion of proportionality that is customized to the context of truth in marketing. For our purposes, proportionality is an operational criterion that determines the normative guidelines that must inform the design of direct and indirect alethic facilitation. Proportionality encompasses four subprinciples: appropriateness; necessity; time-boundedness; and time-endurance.

For a given target group, a suggested course of action is appropriate, if under normal circumstances it will bring about the promised future state of affairs. Appropriateness thereby expresses a sufficient condition for the realization of the product or service property related to a behavioural claim (Anker et al. 2012).

Necessity here is a condition of parsimony that requires a brand to design and facilitate courses of actions that cause the least intrusion into the personal sphere of the consumer. A given course of action, then, is necessary insofar as it belongs to the set of actions that requires the least investment of personal resources (time, effort, commitment) needed to obtain the promised state of affairs/product property. For any given behavioural claim, there may be a range of different courses of actions that will bring about the promised benefit, some of which are very demanding and unnecessary in the sense that other actions may obtain the same property, but at lower effort or in a shorter period of time (i.e., with less investment of personal resources).

Time is a fundamental feature of all human agency and communication (Arundale 1980). Time-boundedness is a very important criterion of behavioural claims because the promised product benefit will only ever occur after continuous consumer–brand interaction over one or more time-sections. Time in organizational and consumptional domains can be subjectively or inter-subjectively constructed or objectively determined (Zaheer, Albert, and Zaheer 1999). Although the subjective time-dimension is crucial to determining the notion of personal investment of resources (e.g., effort) relating to the criterion of necessity, what is of real relevance here is the actual period of time needed in order for the promised product property to emerge from a set of consumer–brand interactions. The focus is therefore on objectively determined time-scales, which the brand needs to adhere to in terms of alethic facilitation. The materialization of behavioral product properties is subject to time-variance: the required consumer time-investment in order for the property to emerge will differ relative to the particular nature of the relevant behavioural property. A behavioural claim is time-bound insofar as it states the approximate period of time the average target consumer should invest in consumer–brand interactions in order to achieve the promised product benefit.

Sometimes alethic facilitation can meet the requirement of time-boundedness and nevertheless fail on the instrumental criterion because the emerging behavioural property is compromised by another temporal problem. The issue is that some behavioural properties may be obtainable by different courses of actions, which will differ in terms of the subsequent durability of the behavioural property. Two courses of action, x_1 and x_2, may both lead to a given behavioural property, X, at a reasonable future point in time, t_1, but whereas X obtained via x_1 will be sustainable over a number of time-sections, $t_1–t_{10}$, X obtained via x_2 ceases to exist at t_2.

The problem is that the behavioural property does not have a reasonable endurance over time. This is not just a theoretical problem: the contemporary marketplace is awash with examples. Perhaps most strikingly are the various offerings that promise consumers substantial weight loss over a short period of time. While it may be possible to lose significant weight within, say, two weeks as many commercial providers promise, the methods needed such as fasting and temporarily cutting out foods that are essential for long-term health mean that any weight loss is likely *not* to be sustainable over time. Evidence finds that long-term weight loss usually requires engaging in high levels of physical activity, eating a low calorie diet and maintaining a consistent eating pattern over time (Wing and Phelan 2005). Structurally identical examples include marketing offerings promising 'Get fit in 2 weeks', 'Improve your confidence in 1 week', or 'Radically change your life today.'

The problem of time endurance is by no means new to the pragmatic theory of truth. James struggles with it, albeit in a much more abstract and hypothetical form. As discussed in Chapter 2, Moore and Russell argue that associating truth with utility is fundamentally flawed, because holding one set of beliefs (say, God exists) may be beneficial to one person but useless to another. And surely, the logical conclusion that God then exists and does not exist qua truth as utility is incoherent and renders the utility-based interpretation of the instrumental criterion of truth unfeasible. Haack (1976) defends James's instrumental criterion of truth against the objection: the notion of utility, she argues, is inseparable from the notion of efficacy *over time* such that a belief that P is useful, only if it is true over time and thereby invulnerable to challenges posed by the acquisition of further beliefs and experiences. This interpretation is consistent with James's (1975b, 106) remark that for something to count as true it must be "expedient in the long run and on the whole". Haack's reflections on time in the pragmatic theory of truth are, structurally, closely related to our present-day cases of behavioural marketing claims. Following Haack, we can formulate the temporal requirement of alethic facilitation as an experiential condition: an emerging behavioural property possesses time-endurance only if the property will not be overthrown by subsequent experience immediately following the emergence of the property.

5.5   When is the consumer entitled to believe a behavioural claim?

Behavioural claims communicate a promise that a given product benefit will emerge if the consumer engages in a specific course of action suggested and facilitated by the brand. The required course of action may be demanding and require significant investment of personal resources such as time or effort. This is, for example, the case when a brand promises to help consumers lead healthy lifestyles, become more sustainable or manage substantial credit card debt. Behavioural claims thereby involve two different types of exchanges: a monetary exchange for a specific product or service, and a resource-based exchange of personal resources. The requirement to engage in a potentially demanding resource-based exchange on top of the monetary exchange implies that consumers should reflect critically on whether the investment of personal resources is worthwhile.

Assuming that the consumer has a strong preference to obtain the promised benefit, the key question is whether the consumer trusts the brand sufficiently to engage in the suggested course of action. In this context, trust is an epistemic concept and signifies the extent to which a communicator (the consumer) is willing to ascribe epistemic authority to another communicator (the brand). Is the brand in a sufficiently strong epistemic situation such that the consumer confidently and willingly engages in the suggested course of action without fear of being misled or ill-advised? Under what circumstances can the consumer trust the brand as epistemic agent authorizing a course of action without being subject to gullibility (Fricker 1994)?

The closely related literature on social epistemology (Goldman and Blanchard 2015), in particular explorations of the epistemological dimension of testimony (Adler 2015), employs the distinction between a priori and a posteriori warrants for acceptance of propositional claims. That distinction is relevant to determining the conditions under which the consumer should critically accept to engage in alethic facilitation that requires resource-based exchanges. Gelfert (2006) argues that communicative agents have an a priori duty to adopt an attitude of trust and honesty towards other communicative agents: a discursive duty not to distrust other people. The rationale – which is an interpretation of Kant's justification of trust as a moral duty (Kant 2012) – is that if we were to systematically distrust all other people, then a ubiquitous breakdown of communications would be inevitable. The reason is that distrust as a default communicative attitude would require that we rigorously check the justification and substantiation of all information communicated to us. This is too high an epistemic standard (Gelfert 2006). Truthfulness is therefore a communicative norm governing everyday social interactions (Fallis 2009, 2012; Grice 1989; Lewis 1969; Schiffer 1972; Searle 1969).

The observation that truthfulness is a presumptive norm in everyday social context motivates the acceptance principle (Burge 1993, 1997).[2] The principle holds that if an agent, A, communicates that P to another agent, B, then B is warranted in accepting P as true, unless there are stronger reasons to the contrary (Burge 1993, 1997). The thrust of the principle is that we are justified in relying on what other people are telling us; that is, it is epistemically permissible to rely on testimonial evidence when acquiring new beliefs, information or assumptions. Before I discuss the acceptance principle in further detail, it is necessary to address the differences between the nature of the domain in which the principle was developed and the particular nature of the social domain of marketing practice to which the principle will here be applied.

The scope of theories of social epistemology and testimony is often constrained to a narrow set of idealized domains in which a number of communicative features characteristic of many, if not most, actual communicative domains are ignored. The domains are theoretically constructed, and core epistemic conditions are controlled such as the degree of knowledge possessed, the purpose of communication and the nature of the units of communication. The theoretical domains constructed for the exploration of pure social epistemology differ from the actual domains of marketing and consumption in at least the following three ways.

First, in the theoretical domains, the receivers (hearers) do not have any special knowledge about the active communicators (speakers) (Adler 2015). This clearly differs from the actual domains of marketing where target audiences normally have some degree of knowledge about the brand or product and in many cases possess significant levels of knowledge. Brand knowledge is assumed to be an antecedent of brand equity (Christodoulides and de Chernatony 2010; Keller 1993, 2001, 2008), and as such brands continuously strive to build, shape and increase consumers' brand beliefs and associations.

Second, the purpose of communication in the controlled, theoretical domains is to inform rather than convince or persuade (Adler 2015). Contrariwise, marketing domains are characterized by incorporating informative, entertaining and persuasive information into a single narrative universe. Persuasive content is hugely important because it has been demonstrated to have significant impact on product demand. Also, consumers' content-sensitivity is reportedly larger than their price-sensitivity in a range of situations (Bertrand et al. 2010).

Third, the units of communication in the controlled, theoretical domains are simple propositions with relatively straightforward truth conditions. By contrast, marketing universes are characterized by a magnitude of complex information, communicating persuasive and informational propositional content via literal (written or spoken), symbolic and visual means of communication.

The persuasive nature of marketing domains is what really sets our context apart from the theoretical domains of pure social epistemology. The main implication is that Gelfert's argument in favour of an a priori, discursive duty to meet communicative agents with trust and thereby, as default epistemic attitude, accept claims as truthful does not apply. The acceptance principle cannot, without qualification, guide communicative agency in the marketing domain because brands have a direct self-serving interest: the overriding aim of businesses is to maximize profits, and all communications are tailored to this end. This means that consumers have to meet marketing communications with an epistemic attitude that is more skeptical and critical than an unqualified Kantian duty to meet others with trust would allow.

A posteriori epistemic warrants

To accommodate the differences in domain ontology it is necessary to augment the acceptance principle with a set of context-specific, a posteriori requirements or epistemic warrants. Fricker (1994, 145) argues that "a hearer should always engage in some assessment of the speaker for trustworthiness". Her suggestion is that communicative agents develop a counterfactual sensitivity through their membership of epistemic communities, which enables them to critically assess somebody's sincerity by ascribing to them probable mental attitudes (beliefs, desires, motivations) and psychological traits. Our ability to competently and confidently ascribe these properties to other people who – in principle – are strangers is based on our interpretive capacity to decode contextual factors. Important contextual factors include likely biases (such as vested interests to be expected from, say, a salesperson who is asked for advice on a product) and person-specific factors (e.g., body language). Whether a speaker is to be trusted is determined by the hearer's contextual-psychological construction of the speaker and her environment.

According to Fricker (1994, 154), the ascription of truth-conducive psychological and contextual properties to a given communicator empowers us to critically assess for trustworthiness:

> This is a matter of the actual engagement of a counterfactual sensitivity: it is true throughout of the hearer that if there were any signs of untrustworthiness, she would pick them up.

Fricker's notion of counterfactual sensitivity is generic and needs to be adapted to the marketing context. Inspired by Fricker's observation that communicators can rely on contextual and agentic cues to make inferences about other communicators' trustworthiness, I will develop a set of contextual epistemic warrants that allow consumers to make workable inferences as to the trustworthiness and veracity of marketing content correlated with behavioural claims. The discussion will revolve around three core themes: reputation; impersonal knowledge as media literacy; and prior plausibility as brand heritage. Where possible, I will progress from standard discussions in social epistemology.

Reputation

The reputations of communicators have a significant impact on receivers' tendency to accept something as true (Adler 2015). Accordingly, if a given communicator, A, has a strong reputation with respect to x state of affairs, then A's communications regarding x will likely be taken as true by audiences familiar with A. Social epistemology has predominantly focused on reputation as a contextual warrant for scientific knowledge in public and academic domains (Adler 2015; Kitcher 2004). Interestingly, the link to marketing is rather strong: reputation plays a predominant role in corporate branding and works as a proxy for corporate trust. Trust, and thereby reputation, is correlated with brand performance, brand loyalty and brand equity (Christodoulides and de Chernatony 2010; Keller 1993, 2001, 2008; Keller, Sternthal, and Tybout 2002).

The main point of interest, however, is that consumers use brand reputation as an epistemic proxy: consumers who trust a given brand will often rely on its reputation as a substitution for checking specific product claims (Chernatony 2006). For example, if a consumer trusts a brand, say, Goodyear's car tyres to be durable and safe, then there is no need to check relevant safety ratings or customer reviews. The consumer thereby uses the reputation of the brand as a proxy for product quality, making redundant the need to check product information. Against this background, I take brand reputation to be a marketing-specific epistemic warrant that allows consumers to trust a brand's alethic facilitation of behavioural claims.

Impersonal knowledge as media literacy

Through education and active participation in epistemically charged social activities (chat, gossip, meetings, conversations, phone calls, etc.), we acquire impersonal knowledge about different types of speakers (Adler 2015). This impersonal knowledge enables us to critically assess other communicators – be it strangers or people we are familiar with – for sincerity and trustworthiness. We know, for example, to interpret hesitance when asking for directions as an epistemic sign of uncertainty, which will influence the extent to which we accept the information as true.

The marketing correlate to impersonal knowledge is, I suggest, media literacy, which Potter (2014) defines as a set of perspectives one can employ to interpret the meaning of mass media messages. Via extensive exposure to various media channels (TV, radio, Internet, games, books, magazines, billboards), numerous types of creative appeals (sex, humour, fear, rational, symbolic, emotional) and different types of content (informative, persuasive, experiential), contemporary citizens in many parts of the world have considerable experience with accessing, interpreting and analyzing media. Moreover, media literacy is a core part of the primary and secondary school curriculum, embedded in subjects such as languages, IT, modern studies, social studies and science. Let us therefore assume that contemporary consumers have a relatively high level of media literacy.

On this assumption, media literacy is an epistemic ability that enables consumers to critically assess the trustworthiness and veracity of propositional claims conveyed via mass media. Media literacy is thereby an epistemic warrant that actualizes Fricker's (1994, 154) notion of counterfactual sensitivity, which involves the notion that "if there were any signs of untrustworthiness, she [the receiver] would pick them up". Thus, if a consumer, C, is media literate, and the given context of communication, X, does not involve any type of subliminal communication or conditioning, then C is warranted in assuming any marketing claim in X to be true on the condition that she finds the claim(s) to be believable.

Prior plausibility as brand heritage

Prior plausibility denotes communicators' ability to determine the trust-worthiness of other communicators' messages based on the credibility or likelihood of the content in a given context. As was the case with impersonal knowledge of different types of speakers, the notion of prior plausibility is strongly associated with communicators' individual epistemic skills and competencies acquired through participation in epistemic communities. However, the object of prior plausibility is propositional content, whereas the object of impersonal knowledge is other communicators. Prior plausibility is a sort of individualized background evidence that works as a filtering device, enabling communicators to quickly and spontaneously determine the probabilistic veracity of propositional content. As Adler (2015, section 6) states, speakers familiar with the climate of Florida will intuitively dismiss as false statements such as "There was a snowstorm in Miami Beach, last July".

The notion of prior plausibility maps well onto the domain of marketing: consumers familiar with a specific product domain, say, smartphones, will easily detect obviously false or unrealistic product claims such as "All functions of the next-generation smartphones will be carried out by thought-control". Similarly, probable propositional content such as "Future smartphone screens will be flexible and bendable" will seem realistic and reasonable. In this example, the assessment of content truthfulness is based on the consumer's familiarity with, and participation in, a specific epistemic-consumptional context.

Pure social epistemology conceptualizes prior plausibility as a context-relative phenomenon. However, for our purposes it is also necessary to formulate an agent-relative version of the concept. In our case, the agent is a brand, and the prior plausibility is established by the brand heritage. This nexus is reasonable because consumers use brand heritage as an indicator of a brand's credibility, reliability and authenticity (Leigh, Peters, and Shelton 2006; Wiedmann et al. 2011). Building on Wiedmann et al. (2011), I conceptualize brand heritage as an interpretation shared by a given social group of a brand's past communications (symbolic, visual and verbal), sustained practices, media exposure over time, and time-stable consumer perceptions in order to establish the communicative trustworthiness of the brand.

Brand heritage thereby becomes a central semantic filter that enables consumers to assess the veracity of marketing communications pertaining to a specific brand. Brand heritage is normatively charged in the sense that, ex hypothesis, it signifies a positive conceptualization of a brand's past.[3] Seminal contributions in the field establish a strong correlation between brand heritage, brand identity, brand image, and brand equity (Aaker 2002; Aaker and Joachimsthaler 2000; Rindell 2013). Brand heritage is an amalgamation of the realization of a brand's core values over time as perceived by the consumer. As such, brand heritage is an indication of reliability and

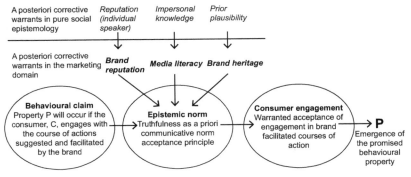

Figure 5.1 Overview of the social epistemological conditions for warranted consumer engagement in brand-facilitated courses of action.

consistency of brand promise delivery over time, and consumers can thereby use brand heritage as a semantic device to filter propositional brand content.

Against this background, I hold that it is warranted for a consumer, C, to accept or reject any given propositional claim, P, from a given brand, X, insofar as C is familiar with X's brand heritage, Z, such that if X claims that P, then C can take P to be true or false given Z.

Figure 5.1 summarizes the social epistemological conditions under which consumers are justified in believing a brand's behavioural claim that a certain product property will emerge, if the consumer adopts X course of action. Social epistemology has established how communicative agents normally operate under a presumptive norm of a priori truthfulness where other agents are trusted by default, unless the context reveals cues that suggest otherwise. However, the strong self-serving interests of brands imply that the marketing context requires some corrective warrants that safeguard the consumer against gullibility. I argue that the notions of brand reputation, media literacy and brand heritage could work as epistemic filters that would enable the consumer to test the veracity of marketing communications.

5.6   A standard objection

I will now return to the classical critique of the instrumental criterion of truth, which I have briefly discussed in Chapter 2 and in this chapter. To recap, Moore (1907) and Russell (1992) disdain the instrumental criterion of truth. Truth, they argue, should not be instrumentally linked to utility because the notion of utility is relative to individual subjects. Holding and acting on a given belief that P (say, the belief that God exists) may prove useful to one person but meaningless to another. Consequently, truth cannot be a matter of instrumental utility unless we accept the skeptical conclusion that truth is subjective and relative. Haack's (1976) solution to the challenge is to argue in favour of a non-subjectivist notion of utility such that holding and acting on a given belief that P is instrumentally true, only if it proves *useful* and *robust* over time in the sense that it will not be overthrown by subsequent experience.

Some may argue (a) that the crux of Moore and Russell's objection applies to the marketing-specific formulation of instrumental truth, and (b) that Haack's rescue attempt is either not convincing or does not apply in the marketing domain. This would then mean (c) that the instrumental criterion of truth in marketing is flawed because it rests on a subjectivist notion of utility.

While Haack offers a defense of the classical pragmatic formulation of truth as usefulness, the theory of truth in marketing escapes the objection by adopting a different notion of instrumentality. In our case, instrumentality is defined relative to the materialization of a promised product benefit, rather than to the usefulness of holding and acting on a robust belief over time. The instrumental definition of truth developed in this chapter holds that a marketing claim is instrumentally true insofar as the promised product benefit occurs as a result of the consumer adopting certain brand-mediated courses of actions. Instrumentality is thereby no longer dependent on any subjective or inter-subjective perceptions of usefulness: it is purely a material condition of the materialization of a property relative to certain external occurrences (i.e., brand-mediated courses of actions adopted by the consumer).

5.7 Conclusion

In summary, behavioural claims promise the consumer the emergence of a property or future state of affairs (e.g., improved health, self-confidence, reduced carbon footprint), which the product- or service-inherent properties cannot materialize. The truth of behavioural claims therefore requires the brand to encourage and facilitate a course of action that, if adopted by the consumer, will bring about the promised behavioural property. I dubbed this process alethic facilitation, which can take a direct or indirect form. Alethic facilitation has to be carefully targeted because some behavioural properties associated with everyday products (e.g., performance-enhancing sports drinks) may only hold true for a very narrow target group (e.g., professional athletes), to which the average and intended consumer does not belong.

Instrumental truth materializes in consumer–brand interactions, and both parties thereby hold a shared alethic responsibility. Dual responsibility is the case even when the consumer is under the influence of persuasive marketing and a given product desire has been induced through exposure to marketing. The reason is that lack of doxastic control does not entail lack of behavioural control. This means that the consumer is at liberty to decide to accept or decline any interaction with the brand. The shared alethic responsibility also means that if the consumer decides to engage in brand-facilitated

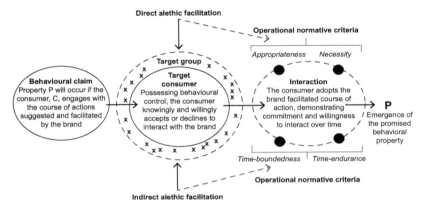

Figure 5.2 Conceptual model of the truth of behavioural claims in marketing.

courses of action, then she commits herself to engage wholeheartedly, with commitment and willingness to interact with the brand for a period of time long enough for the behavioural property to emerge.

When facilitating courses of action designed to bring about behavioural properties, brands place themselves under an ethical obligation to meet certain normative standards. In particular, alethic facilitation has to meet the four-fold criterion of proportionality, ensuring that the suggested courses of action are appropriate, necessary, time-bound and time-endurant. If the alethic facilitation is properly designed and the consumer engages with commitment and effort over time, then the promised product property will, under normal circumstances, materialize within a reasonable time horizon. Figure 5.2 summarizes the truth-making process with regard to behavioural claims in marketing.

Notes

1 This argument builds on Dewey's understanding of beliefs as habits of action: instrumental truth is to hold a belief that grounds a pattern of behaviour, which produces successful outcomes over time.
2 The acceptance principle is also referred to as the default rule (Bach 1984) or the PR (presumptive right) thesis (Fricker 1994).
3 It is reasonable to object that brand heritage may be negatively charged. For example, consumers would most likely form a negative perception of a brand's actions over time if it consistently broke its promises, deceived consumers and sold products of an unacceptable standard. However, extant research has established brand heritage as an intrinsically valuable entity, meaning that the concept, by definition, is *positively normatively charged*. Brand *history* can be used to address a brand's actions over time with a neutral or negative value.

6   Alethic pluralism

> Some things come in more than one form: there is more than one way for a friendship to flourish, for a person to be beautiful, and for a life to be fulfilling. *Alethic pluralism* applies this thought to truth: there is more than one way for a proposition to be true.
>
> Michael P. Lynch, *Truth and Multiple Realizability*

6.1   The pluralistic nature of the theory of truth in marketing

So far I have avoided the question of what kind of theory the theory of truth in marketing is. The time has now come to say a few words on this meta-theoretical issue. Theories of truth can be divided into three very rough camps: deflationism, monism and pluralism.

Deflationists are not exactly skeptics about truth, but they come close. They hold that truth is a non-informative phenomenon that amounts to no more than the observation that P is true if and only if 'P'. That is all there is to say because to assert that a statement is true is to assert the statement itself (Stoljar and Damnjanovic 2014). Truth is thereby reduced to a logical device for expressing general statements that apply to infinite chains of propositions (Lynch 2015). Consequently, the concept of truth is void of any substantial property and thereby unable to act as an explanatory vehicle.

Monism is the view that there is one – and just one – property by virtue of which propositional claims are true. All claims, regardless of their type or the nature of the domain over which they predicate, are alethically the same: it is the same quality – correspondence with facts *or* coherence with other beliefs *or* the instrumental value of holding and acting on a belief, *or* ... – that turn a statement true.

In one respect, truth pluralism is closely associated with monism in that both positions are *substantive accounts of truth*. Both monism and pluralism agree that statements about the world are true or false because there is some substantial cross-categorial feature external to the statement itself that makes the statement true or false. But contrary to monism, pluralism argues in favour of the existence of two or more alethic properties, that is,

that there is more than one unique feature about the world that makes statements true or false.

Motivated by deflationism's sustained attack on the very concept of truth
and the subsequent popularity of the position in mainstream epistemology,
alethic pluralism has seen a surge of creative interest in contemporary epistemology. Seminal contributions include Lynch (1998, 2004, 2009, 2013),
Pedersen (2006, 2010), Edwards (2011, 2013), C. D. Wright (2005, 2010),
C. Wright (2013) and Wright and Pedersen (2010b). For an overview of the
contemporary debate, see Pedersen (2012).[1]

The theory of truth in marketing is obviously a pluralistic theory of truth,
triangulating correspondence, coherence and instrumentalism. Alethic pluralism is not a homogeneous group of theories, but rather comprises a number of different views on truth (Wright 2013). However, the main feature of
pluralism is often portrayed like this (Pedersen and Wright 2013, 2):

> Although there are various ways to articulate the core pluralist thesis,
> it has typically been construed thus: what property makes propositions
> true may vary across domains, or from subject matter to subject matter.

One can cash out this general description of alethic pluralism in many different ways, and I shall now clarify the pluralistic nature of the theory of
truth in marketing.

The quoted description of pluralism as the view that truth-makers are
domain-relative seems to tacitly assume that propositions only range
over content within one specified domain. In one way, this makes sense.
For example, the alethic features of mathematical statements (such as the
Peano axioms that define the arithmetic properties of natural numbers) are
limited to the overall domain of mathematics and have no alethic meaning
outside this domain. Mathematical statements may, of course, appear outside the domain of mathematics: a comedian may treat a mathematical subject matter, but this domain of entertainment is not truth-relevant. Or, to be
precise, it is not truth-relevant with respect to mathematical truths. It may
very well be relevant in terms of an exploration of the nature of truth in fiction, but this is another story belonging to another domain. And the nature
of truth in fiction is potentially entirely different from the nature of truth in
mathematics, and it is in this sense that truth-values vary across domains.

The pluralistic nature of truth in marketing is of a different nature, however. In this context, we are dealing with one specified domain, which features
different types of statements (functional, symbolic and behavioural) that
are true in virtue of radically different alethic properties (correspondence,
coherence, instrumentality). Here, then, alethic pluralism is *not* characterized by different alethic properties belonging to different domains, but by
the same domain comprising three different types of alethic properties.
For the purposes of this study, I propose the following definition.

Alethic pluralism in the marketing domain
Truth pluralism is the view that the domain of marketing features a set of
different truth-makers, which are capable of explaining and determining the
veracity of different types of marketing claims. The truth-makers are substantially different such that no monistic theory can explain them all.

The next section's discussion of relativism will further refine the theory's
pluralistic stance.

6.2   Alethic pluralism and objectivity

Relativism is the most pressing problem for alethic pluralism. The problem
goes like this. On the one hand, pluralism about truth is deeply rooted in
basic observations of the world: in this study, for example, we have seen
multiple times how different accounts of truth *can* explain the veracity of
different types of claims. Moreover, a multifocal lens of truth is *necessary*
because the truth properties of the different types of claims are analyzable
only in terms of different theories of truth.

On the other hand, the explanatory power gained from developing a conceptual scheme that employs multiple views of truth, critics argue, is deeply
flawed because alethic pluralism entails relativism about truth. And, as Lynch
(1998) remarks, opponents to pluralism argue that truth relativism entails
truth nihilism. The argument takes the following form: if we grant alethic
pluralism, then we submit to the view that there could, and often would, be
more than one true description of any given state of the world. Thus, on one
theory, T_1, description P of x state of affairs in the external world would be
true, while on another theory, T_2, description Q of x would be true. The intuitive attraction of alethic pluralism deflates when relativism collapses into
nihilism, which would happen if our two descriptions, P and Q, are incompatible. Given the potential infinite plurality of conceptual schemes, there
are no metaphysical constraints that would prevent this from happening. The
consequence is that we end up in a situation with two or more theories that
both produce true – but incompatible – descriptions of the same aspect of the
world. This violates any rational account of truth and, therefore, renders the
very concept of truth unattainable. Truth nihilism is unavoidable.

The problem of truth nihilism is not just of abstract metaphysical concern. It has direct practical bearing on applied domains. Opponents could
use the hard case discussed above (where the application of the correspondence and coherence criteria to the ads that the ASA found to sexualize a
child would provide competing and irreconcilable versions of truth) as an
example of how nihilism materializes through incompatible truths in practical discourse. Applied epistemologists cannot afford to ignore the problem.

Kantian constructivism and logical pluralism

There are two different responses open to the alethic pluralist. I call the first response Kantian constructivism because it relies on Kant's notion of *synthetic* a priori structuring of human experience and cognition. The basic idea is that human experience will always be structured in a certain way by our epistemic categories. For example, our experience of the external world is tempo-spatial because our cognitive make-up makes us perceive the world through time and space. But it is perfectly possible, Kant argues, that epistemic cognition of the world could be structured differently: it is logically possible for a being to perceive the world as timeless, for example. We humans are epistemically hardwired to experience the world through certain epistemic categories, but we could have been wired differently.

The relativistic challenge can now be tackled: truth is plural in the sense that other radically different experiences of the same fact are possible. But at the same time, truth is fundamentally non-relative because all humans are epistemologically hardwired in exactly the same way such that it is a universal fact that all human beings will necessarily experience the world through the same epistemic categories (e.g., as a tempo-spatial externality). Kantian constructivism is a form of logical pluralism that ensures strong global objectivism (truth is de facto explained by the same property across all domains, given the universally shared epistemic make-up). I define the position thus:

Logical pluralism and strong global objectivism (Kantian constructivism)

- There is a set of epistemic categories that *necessarily* structure all human experience in a certain way across all actual domains, but it is *logically possible* that our epistemic categories could have been different.
- Truth-makers are thus stable across all actual domains (global objectivism), but each domain could have featured alternate truth-makers (logical pluralism).

However, Kantian constructivism is not a viable solution to the challenge of relativism in our case because marketing is faced with *substantial* pluralism that materializes in practical domains, and not just the theoretically possible *logical* pluralism.[2]

Conceptual schemes and substantial pluralism

The second way of responding to the relativistic challenge is to employ the notion of conceptual schemes (Lynch 1998). Epistemic agents who are active in different domains may have different conceptual schemes, which ultimately produce differing accounts of truth. Conceptual schemes are the epistemic lenses through which we experience the world. They comprise large sets of assumptions about the structure of the world; cultural and professional values; normative principles that guide our behaviours and fuel our judgements; and beliefs and concepts that shape our representation of the entire world. As such, conceptual schemes are epistemic devices that give rise to the existence of different world-views.[3]

Now, conceptual schemes may differ from domain to domain such that epistemic agents situated in two different domains may have substantially different alethic perceptions of the same external reality. A given state of affairs, x, in the external world may be true in virtue of C_1 criterion of truth in one domain, D_1, whereas x in the neighbouring domain, D_2, is true in terms of the competing criterion C_2. This amounts to *substantial* pluralism because the existence of competing accounts of truth, C_1 and C_2, is not merely a logical possibility, but an actual epistemic occurrence in the onto-logical worlds of D_1 and D_2.

This understanding of conceptual schemes allows us to develop two different lines of response to the relativistic challenge.

On the one hand, conceptual schemes may fluctuate from domain to domain but nevertheless share one cross-domain alethic property. Fumerton (2013) makes the case that the correspondence theory of truth can accommodate the driving intuitions underpinning alethic pluralism by explaining truth-variances on a representational continuum. Although Fumerton argues forcefully against the idea of employing more than one theory of truth (and in that sense is not a substantive but merely a representational pluralist), his pluralistic conceptuali-zation of correspondence motivates the idea that there exists a cross-domain alethic property that could ensure the compatibility of substantive pluralism and global objectivism. Let me hash out the idea in greater detail.

Different conceptual schemes would feature genuinely different alethic properties such that the same external reality would be true in virtue of different criteria in different domains. But at the same time there would be one overarching alethic property (e.g., correspondence) such that any given fact in the world is analyzable in terms of that alethic property (though not exhaustively). Correspondence would then work as a super-imposing ale-thic property, which would enjoy the sole privilege of ranging over all actual and possible domains. Truth thereby fluctuates from domain to domain, but there is a considerable level of cross-domain alethic stability provided by correspondence. We can now make a claim to objectivity and universality in the face of pluralism.

Where Kantian constructivism is a form of *strong* global objectivism, the solution just outlined amounts to *modest* universalism: there is only *one* universal alethic property, whereas Kantian constructivism ensures that all alethic properties are – or would be – operationally universal. The modest solution to relativism can be formulated thus:

Substantive pluralism and modest global objectivism

- For any domain, there exists a unique conceptual scheme with one shared epistemic feature such that all truth-relevant experience is necessarily structured differently across all domains, with the exception of one cross-domain epistemic characteristic.
- Two types of truth-makers are thus active in any domain. First is domain-relative truth-makers that are stable within any given domain (local objectivism), but vary across domains (substantive pluralism). Second is a shared cross-domain truth-maker that is active in all epistemic contexts (modest global objectivism).

The chief concern with the modest solution is to provide a convincing argument as to why there should be such a thing as an alethically privileged property that ranges over all domains in an epistemic environment featuring a multitude of alethic properties. And even if advocates of the position should succeed, the problem of demonstrating why one specific alethic property should enjoy supremacy still remains. On what grounds should we choose, say, correspondence over coherence or instrumentality, seeing that they are all fundamental alethic properties? It is difficult to see how to solve this situation without invoking a normative principle. The next problem would then be to justify the alethic relevance of that principle.

The claim to universality is genuinely appealing in pure science as it strives for maximum generalizability, but the question is whether it is necessary and desirable in applied domains. I think not.

Integrating modest global objectivism into the pluralistic framework is not necessary with regard to truth in marketing: we are only concerned with the veracity of marketing claims within the marketing domain and thus do not have an operational need for cross-domain alethic comparisons, rendering modest global objectivism practically irrelevant. Moreover, as each type of claim (functional, symbolic, behavioural) by default is assigned to a specific alethic property (correspondence, coherence, instrumentality), the very concept of alethic primacy is not operational either. The alethic criteria will by definition not be competing against each other as they each range over clearly delineated sectors within the overall domain. Consequently, all that is needed is local objectivism.

My reply to the relativistic challenge is therefore to adopt substantive pluralism but to discard any claim to alethic generalizability across differing conceptual schemes. Truth is stable within any given conceptual scheme: the relevant epistemic agents (e.g., marketers, consumers, advertising regulators, marketing scholars) are not at liberty to change the alethic configuration of the scheme. On the contrary, the conceptual scheme works as an epistemic constraint that determines what truth is for any given agent within the domain. Accordingly, the theory of truth in marketing rests on the following definition of pluralism, which provides the metaphysically least demanding solution to the relativistic challenge:

Substantive pluralism and local objectivism

- For any domain, there exists a unique conceptual scheme such that all human experience is necessarily structured differently across domains.
- Truth-makers are stable within any given domain (local objectivism) but vary across domains (substantive pluralism).

Figure 6.1 summarizes the discussion of the relativistic challenge by representing the three different conceptual schemes that underpin the alethic variations of pluralism.

A threat to local objectivism

As discussed, local objectivism does not allow the attribution of supremacy to any alethic property. This is an advantage in terms of providing a domain ontology that is metaphysically more economic and sustainable: there is no

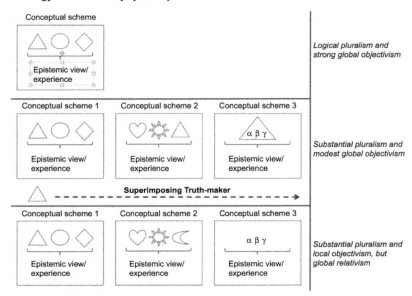

Figure 6.1 Overview of how three conceptual schemes give rise to logical and substantive pluralism and produce variations of alethic objectivism.

need to identify a robust normative-epistemic principle to justify why one alethic property is more important than another. However, the absence of a super-imposing alethic property that ranges over all domains makes local objectivism susceptible to 'alethic erosion'. By this I mean that epistemically privileged agents – such as adjudicators like the ASA – may influence the content of the alethic criteria and the conditions under which they are operative. This puts local objectivism under threat: if one group of privileged epistemic agents can influence what is true within a given domain, then truth is not objective but inter-subjectively determined by an elite group of people. This makes truth relative. And then the theory collapses back into truth nihilism.

Again, this is not just a metaphysically interesting problem, but an issue that lies at the heart of marketing practice. When an adjudicator and watchdog like the ASA makes a ruling, for example stating that a claim is unsubstantiated or untrue, then its verdict represents the truth. As the ASA has the power to ban marketing campaigns, the regulator is in possession of both epistemic and pragmatic power: by making a ruling, they implicitly state what is true; by enforcing it, they make the verdict a tangible truth with practical implications for marketing practice.

Although any adjudicator is clearly not at liberty to change legislation, regulations or codes on a whim, any adjudication involves a degree of interpretation. The underpinning truth criteria are thereby not entirely stable. And local objectivism provides no overriding truth criterion that can be used to reset any criteria altered via the adjudicator's interpretations to their default positions. To address this problem, local objectivism needs to introduce some form of truth-stabilization. And this is exactly what the ASA has done.

When the ASA receives a complaint, it assesses the case against the relevant codes of conduct (i.e., the CAP codes). Sometimes the codes are easy to apply to the case, and the Council (the jury) makes a decision to uphold, partly uphold or reject the complaint. In more complex cases, the Council calls on external experts to interpret the evidence and may ask for advice from other national or international regulators. Furthermore, a designated member of the senior management team, the Head of Casework, is responsible for ensuring consistency of regulatory decision making. The Council then makes a decision in light of this external advice.

Put differently, when the Council is in doubt as to what the right decision is – that is, when there is doubt as to what the truth about a given ad is – it will consult external experts who have an epistemically privileged view on the matter. The final judgement – the established truth about the ad – is then a result of the Council's interpretation of the codes, informed by the qualified opinion of designated external epistemic agents. In effect, the employment of external experts ensures objectivity, professionalism and impartiality and is thereby a form of truth-stabilization within the context of alethic pluralism and local objectivism.[4] Figure 6.2 describes how the ASA ensures objectivity of judgement.

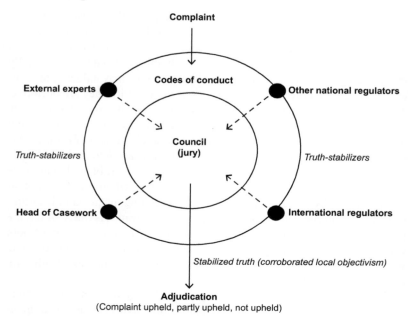

Figure 6.2 The employment of truth-stabilizers to ensure the objectivity of judgements within the framework of alethic pluralism and local objectivism.

6.3   Truth and normativity

The final question of this exploration addresses alethic normativity: is truth a neutral or value-laden concept?

On the face of it, truth is about what there *is*, whereas morality is about what there *should be*. Indeed, advocates of the correspondence theory of truth could argue convincingly along those lines. However, the boundaries between the descriptive and normative realms are blurred and overlapping. As Kripke (1982, 37) observes:

> Suppose I do mean addition by '+'. What is the relation of this supposition to the question how I will respond to the problem '68+57'? The dispositionalist gives a *descriptive* account of this relation: if '+' meant addition, then I will answer '125'. But this is not the proper account of the relation, which is *normative*, not descriptive. The point is *not* that, if I meant addition by '+', I *will* answer '125', but that, if I intend to accord with my past meaning of '+', I *should* answer '125'. ... The relation of meaning and intention to future action is *normative*, not *descriptive*.

There is considerable current interest in normative epistemology (Andler 2000; Boghossian 2003; Kornblith 1993; Lockard 2013; Lynch 2015). The debate focuses chiefly on whether truth grounds cognitive values that epistemic agents *should* adhere to in their various undertakings. Those arguing that truth is indeed a value can then distinguish between two normative functions (Lynch 2015): truth as a *norm* (beliefs are correct when they are true); and truth as a *goal* (truth is valuable to science and societal practice and should therefore be the goal of many of our actions).

Truth may be the goal of marketing science (Hunt 1990), but it will never be the goal of marketing practice. But surely, truth is a norm in marketing: the book opened with a reference to marketing codes of conduct, stressing that marketing should be truthful, honest and non-deceptive. The question then is in what sense is truth a norm in marketing.

The normativity of truth is often discussed under the banners of 'meaning-normativity' or 'content-normativity' (Boghossian 2003; Glüer and Wikforss 2015; Whiting 2007). The central assumption – captured by the preceding Kripke quote – is that meaningful expressions are correlated with correctness-conditions that shape and guide epistemic processes (such as belief acquisition and revision) (Glüer and Wikforss 2015). Meaningful content is never value-neutral, presumably because our actions are fundamentally goal-directed. Meaning is always associated with intention, and intention expresses a desire for something to change: for a person to have an intention to x, is to have a desire and be motivated to bring about x state of affairs. Meaning is thus correlated with an endeavor to make the world into what it *should* be, from a given intentional point of view.

Marketing represents a special case in terms of alethic normativity: undeniably, marketing content is by definition normative, as its very purpose is to persuade consumers to buy stuff. But this is neither solely nor primarily a matter of epistemic normativity: it is a moral matter. We – consumers, customers, regulators – expect marketers to be truthful! We can explain this expectation – and thereby how truth becomes ethically charged – by connecting to Andler's (2000) discussion of *context*-normativity as opposed to *content*-normativity. The upshot of the discussion is that "the context dictates, or at least constrains, the proper accomplishment of the act (Andler 2000, 273).

This makes perfect sense for marketing: what transforms truth from being a purely epistemic value into an ethical requirement is the fact that truth is laid down as a fundamental ground rule of marketing practice through regulation and codes of conducts. Truth in marketing is thereby not just a question of whether or not some piece of information is substantiated: truth is the ultimate moral norm of marketing practice dictated by the societal context.

6.4   Conclusion

The chapter opened with a broad distinction between three different types of alethic theories (monism, pluralism, deflationism) and provided a concise definition of alethic pluralism as employed in this exploration. Here, alethic pluralism is the view (a) that the marketing domain comprises a set of different truth-makers, which explain the veracity of different types of marketing claims; and (b) that truth-makers are *not* analyzable in terms of a single theory of truth.

Alethic pluralism is a theoretically demanding position: due to its relativistic nature, the theory's opponents argue that it necessarily slips into subjectivism and nihilism. Nothing prevents scenarios where two different theories provide true, but mutually incompatible, accounts of the same phenomenon. Alethic pluralism is thereby an incoherent, self-refuting theory of truth. I discussed three different solutions to the relativistic challenge and argued in favour of substantive pluralism, combined with local objectivism. This is the view (a) that different conceptual schemes are operational in different domains; *and* (b) that alethic criteria fluctuate relative to conceptual schemes, *but* (c) remain stable within the parameters of the relevant conceptual scheme and domain of application. This stance solves the relativistic challenge by ensuring local objectivism.

The final section ventured into the relationship between truth and normativity. Having distinguished between epistemic and ethical normativity, truth in marketing was shown to be the ultimate moral requirement because regulations and codes of conducts define truthfulness as the bedrock of marketing ethics.

Notes

1   *Truth and Pluralism* (Pedersen and Wright 2013) is the first collected volume to provide a series of topical papers from the most influential alethic pluralists.
2   Note that Lynch (1998) develops a certain interpretation of Kantianism, which is combined with substantial alethic pluralism.
3   Conceptual schemes are a bit like Kantian synthetic a priori categories of experience in the sense that the experiences of any individual epistemic agent will necessarily be shaped by a conceptual scheme. The fundamental difference is that conceptual schemes are a posteriori, rather than a priori, because they are grounded in domain-relative experiences.
4   Pedersen (2010) addresses another notion of truth-stabilization of alethic pluralism. There, the aim is to demonstrate that alethic pluralism can defeat 'the instability challenge', which is an argument that refutes pluralism by demonstrating that the position is logically committed to alethic uniformity, that is, the view that truth properties remain stable across domains.

References

Aaker, David A., and Erich Joachimsthaler. 2000. *Brand Leadership*. New York: Free Press.

Aaker, David A. 2002. *Building Strong Brands*. London: Free Business Press.

Adler, Jonathan. 2015. "Epistemological Problems of Testimony." In *Stanford Encyclopedia of Philosophy*, Edward N. Zalta (ed.). Stanford, CA: Stanford University. Accessed February 8, 2016. http://plato.stanford.edu/archives/sum2015/entries/testimony-episprob.

Alexy, Robert. 2002. *A Theory of Constitutional Rights*. Translated by J. Rivers. Oxford, UK: Oxford University Press.

Alexy, Robert. 2003. "Constitutional Rights, Balancing, and Rationality." *Ratio Juris* 16 (2):130–140. doi: 10.1111/1467-9337.00228.

Andler, Daniel. 2000. "The Normativity of Context." *Philosophical Studies* 100 (3):273–303. doi: 10.1023/A:1018628709589.

Anker, Thomas Boysen, Linda Brennan, and Dorthe Brogård Kristensen. 2015. "Truth in Social Marketing: Applying Truth Frameworks to the Strategic Evaluation of Social Marketing Campaigns." World Social Marketing Conference, Sydney, Australia, April 19–21.

Anker, Thomas Boysen, Klemens Kappel, Douglas Eadie, and Peter Sandøe. 2012. "Fuzzy Promises – Explicative Definitions of Brand Promise Delivery." *Marketing Theory* 12 (3):267–287. doi: 10.1177/1470593112451379.

Anker, Thomas Boysen, Peter Sandøe, Tanja Kamin, and Klemens Kappel. 2011. "Health Branding Ethics." *Journal of Business Ethics* 104 (1):33–45. doi: 10.1007/s10551-011-0887-9.

Anker, Thomas Boysen, Leigh Sparks, Luiz Moutinho, and Christian Grönroos. 2015. "Consumer Dominant Value Creation: A Theoretical Response to the Recent Call for a Consumer Dominant Logic for Marketing." *European Journal of Marketing* 49 (3/4):532–560. doi: 10.1108/EJM-09-2013-0518.

Apel, Karl-Otto. 1980. "C. S. Peirce and the Post-Tarskian Problem of an Adequate Explication of the Meaning of Truth, Part I." *The Monist* 63 (3):386–407. doi: 10.5840/monist198063323.

Apel, Karl-Otto. 1982. "C. S. Peirce and the Post-Tarskian Problem of an Adequate Explication of the Meaning of the Truth: Towards a Transcendental-Pragmatic Theory of Truth, Part II." *Transactions of the Charles S. Peirce Society* 18 (1):3–17. doi: 10.2307/40319946.

Aquinas, Thomas. 1954. *Truth*. Translated by Robert W. Mulligan. Vol. 1–3. Indianapolis, IN: Hackett Publishing Company.

Aquinas, Thomas. 2006. *Summa Theologiae*. Cambridge, UK: Cambridge University Press.

Armstrong, David M. 1991. "Classes Are States of Affairs." *Mind* 100 (2):189–200. doi: 10.1093/mind/C.398.189.

Armstrong, David M. 1997. *A World of States of Affairs*. Cambridge, UK: Cambridge University Press.

Armstrong, David M. 2004. *Truth and Truthmakers*. Cambridge, UK: Cambridge University Press.

Arnould, Eric J., and Craig J. Thompson. 2005. "Consumer Culture Theory (CCT): Twenty Years of Research." *Journal of Consumer Research* 31 (4):868–882. doi: 10.1086/426626.

Arundale, Robert B. 1980. "Studying Change over Time: Criteria for Sampling from Continuous Variables." *Communication Research* 7 (2):227–263. doi: 10.1177/009365028000700204.

ASA (Advertising Standards Authority). 2010. ASA Ruling on Yoga Alliance UK.

ASA (Advertising Standards Authority). 2011a. ASA Ruling on Ferrero UK Ltd.

ASA (Advertising Standards Authority). 2011b. ASA Ruling on Unilever UK Ltd.

ASA (Advertising Standards Authority). 2012a. Adjudication on American Apparel (UK) Ltd.

ASA (Advertising Standards Authority). 2012b. ASA Ruling on American Apparel (UK) Ltd.

ASA (Advertising Standards Authority). 2012c. ASA Ruling on Incognito.

ASA (Advertising Standards Authority). 2014a. Adjudication on Johnson & Johnson Ltd.

ASA (Advertising Standards Authority). 2014b. ASA Ruling on The Disney Store Ltd.

ASA (Advertising Standards Authority). 2015a. ASA Ruling on American Apparel (UK) Ltd.

ASA (Advertising Standards Authority). 2015b. ASA Ruling on Prada SpA.

ASA (Advertising Standards Authority). 2015c. ASA Ruling on Unibet (International) Ltd.

Atlas, Jay David. 2005. *Logic, Meaning, and Conversation: Semantical Underdeterminacy, Implicature, and Their Interface*. Oxford, UK: Oxford University Press.

Attas, Daniel. 1999. "What's Wrong with "Deceptive" Advertising?" *Journal of Business Ethics* 21 (1):49–59. doi: 10.1023/A:1005985723779.

Audi, Robert. 2011. *Epistemology: A Contemporary Introduction to the Theory of Knowledge*. New York: Routledge.

Austin, Erica, Weintraub, Yi-Chun "Yvonnes" Chen, Bruce E. Pinkleton, and Jessie Quintero Johnson. 2006. "Benefits and Costs of Channel One in a Middle School Setting and the Role of Media-Literacy Training." *Pediatrics* 117 (3):e423–e433. doi: 10.1542/peds.2005–0953.

Austin, John L. 1950. "Truth." *Proceedings of the Aristotelian Society, Supplementary Volumes* 24:111–128. doi: 10.2307/4106745.

Bach, Kent. 1984. "Default Reasoning: Jumping to Conclusions and Knowing When to Think Twice." *Pacific Philosophical Quarterly* 65 (1):37–58.

Baudrillard, Jean. 1981. *For a Critique of the Political Economy of the Sign*. St Louis, MO: Telos Press.

Baudrillard, Jean. 1994. *Simulacra and Simulation*. Ann Arbor: University of Michigan Press.

Baudrillard, Jean. 1998. *The Consumer Society: Myths and Structures*. London: SAGE.

BBC. 2012. *The Truth About Sports Products*. BBC One, Panorama, July 19.

Beebee, Helen, and Julian Dodd. 2005a. "Introduction." In *Truthmakers: The Contemporary Debate*, edited by Helen Beebee and Julian Dodd, 1–16. Oxford, UK: Oxford University Press.

Beebee, Helen, and Julian Dodd, eds. 2005b. *Truthmakers: The Contemporary Debate*. Oxford, UK: Oxford University Press.

Bender, John W. 1989. *The Current State of the Coherence Theory, Philosophical Studies Series*. Dordrecht: Kluwer Academic Publishers.

Bernard, Robert, and Terence Horgan. 2013. "The Synthetic Unity of Truth." In *Truth and Pluralism*, edited by Nikolaj J. L. L. Pedersen and Cory D. Wright, 180–196. Oxford, UK: Oxford University Press.

Bertrand, Marianne, Dean Karlan, Sendhil Mullainathan, Eldar Shafir, and Jonathan Zinman. 2010. "What's Advertising Content Worth? Evidence from a Consumer Credit Marketing Field Experiment." *The Quarterly Journal of Economics* 125 (1):263–306. doi: 10.1162/qjec.2010.125.1.263.

Bhat, Subodh, and Srinivas K. Reddy. 1998. "Symbolic and Functional Positioning of Brands." *Journal of Consumer Marketing* 15 (1):32–43. doi:10.1108/07363769810202664.

Bigelow, John. 1988. *The Reality of Numbers: A Physicalist's Philosophy of Mathematics*. Oxford, UK: Oxford University Press.

Birdsell, David S., and Leo Groarke. 2007. "Outlines of a Theory of Visual Argument." *Argumentation and Advocacy: The Journal of the American Forensic Association* 43 (3–4):103–113.

Blair, J. Anthony. 2012. "The Rhetoric of Visual Arguments." In *Groundwork in the Theory of Argumentation*, edited by Christopher W. Tindale, 261–279. Springer Netherlands.

Blanshard, Brand. 1939. *The Nature of Thought*. London: Allen & Unwin.

Boghossian, Paul A. 2003. "The Normativity of Content." *Philosophical Issues* 13 (1):31–45. doi: 10.1111/1533–6077.00003.

BonJour, Laurence. 1985. *The Structure of Empirical Knowledge*. Cambridge, MA: Harvard University Press.

Bothwell, Claire. 2005. "Burberry Versus the Chavs." BBC. Accessed September 8, 2015. http://news.bbc.co.uk/1/hi/business/4381140.stm.

Bourdieu, Pierre. 1984. *Distinction: A Social Critique of the Judgment of Taste*. Translated by Richard Nice. London: Routledge & Kegan Paul.

Bourdieu, Pierre. 1998. *Practical Reason: On the Theory of Action*. Oxford, UK: Polity.

Bradley, Francis Herbert. 1914. *Essays on Truth and Reality*. Oxford, UK: Clarendon Press.

Buckingham, David. 2006. *Media Education: Literacy, Learning and Contemporary Culture*. Cambridge, UK: Policy Press.

Burge, Tyler. 1993. "Content Preservation." *The Philosophical Review* 102 (4):457–488. doi: 10.2307/2185680.

Burge, Tyler. 1997. "Interlucution, Perception, and Memory." *Philosophical Studies* 86 (1):21–47. doi: 10.1023/A:1004261628340.

Carrington, Michal J., Benjamin A. Neville, and Gregory J. Whitwell. 2010. "Why Ethical Consumers Don't Walk Their Talk: Towards a Framework for Understanding the Gap Between the Ethical Purchase Intentions and Actual Buying Behaviour of Ethically Minded Consumers." *Journal of Business Ethics* 97 (1):139–158. doi: 10.1007/s10551–010–0501–6.

Chernatony, Leslie de. 2006. *From Brand Vision to Brand Evaluation*. Oxford, UK: Butterworth-Heinemann.

Christodoulides, George, and Leslie de Chernatony. 2010. "Consumer-Based Brand Equity Conceptualisation and Measurement." *International Journal of Market Research* 52 (1):43–66. doi: 10.2501/S1470785310201053.

Cohen, Deborah. 2012. "The Truth about Sports Drinks." *British Medical Journal* 345:e4737. doi: 10.1136/bmj.e4737.

Cormier, Harvey. 2001. *The Truth Is What Works: William James, Pragmatism, and the Seed of Death*. Boston: Rowman & Littlefield.

Cupchik, Gerald. 2001. "Constructivist Realism: An Ontology That Encompasses Positivist and Constructivist Approaches to the Social Sciences." *Forum: Qualitative Social Research* 2 (1):1–12.

Dancy, Jonathan. 1998. *Introduction to Contemporary Epistemology*. Oxford, UK: Blackwell.

David, Marian. 2005. "Armstrong on Truthmaking." In *Truthmakers: The Contemporary Debate*, edited by Helen Beebee and Julian Dodd, 141–159. Oxford, UK: Oxford University Press.

David, Marian. 2015. "The Correspondence Theory of Truth." In *Stanford Encyclopedia of Philosophy*, Edward N. Zalta (ed.). Stanford, CA: Stanford University. Accessed February 8, 2016. http://plato.stanford.edu/archives/fall2015/entries/truth-correspondence.

Davidson, Donald. 1969. "True to the Facts." *The Journal of Philosophy* 66 (21):748–764. doi: 10.2307/2023778.

Davidson, Donald. 1986. "A Coherence Theory of Truth and Knowledge." In *Truth and Interpretation: Perspectives on the Philosophy of Donald Davidson*, edited by Ernest LePore, 307–319. Oxford: Blackwell.

Davidson, Donald. 1990. "The Structure and Content of Truth." *The Journal of Philosophy* 87 (6):279–328. doi: 10.2307/2026863.

Descartes, René. 1991. *The Philosophical Writings of Descartes*. Vol. 3. Cambridge, UK: Cambridge University Press.

Descartes, René. 2013. *Meditations on First Philosophy: with Selections from the Objections and Replies*. Edited by John Cottingham. New York: Cambridge University Press.

Dodd, Julian. 2002. "Is Truth Supervenient on Being?" *Proceedings of the Aristotelian Society* 102 (1):69–85. doi: 10.1111/j.0066–7372.2003.00043.x.

Douven, Igor, and Wouter Meijs. 2007. "Measuring Coherence." *Synthese* 156 (3):405–425. doi: 10.1007/s11229–006–9131-z.

Dove. 2015. "The Dove Campaign for Real Beauty." Accessed December 9, 2015. http://www.dove.us/Social-Mission/campaign-for-real-beauty.aspx.

Durkheim, Emile. 1982. *The Rules of Sociological Method*. Translated by W. D. Halls: Macmillan Press.

Dworkin, Gerald. 1982. "Law as Interpretation." *Critical Inquiry* 9 (1):179–200.

Economist. 2011. "Burberry and Globalisation: A Checkered Story." *The Economist*. Accessed September 8, 2015. http://www.economist.com/node/17963363.

Edwards, Douglas. 2011. "Simplyfying Alethic Pluralism." *The Southern Journal of Philosophy* 49 (1):28–48. doi: 10.1111/j.2041–6962.2010.00043.x.

Edwards, Douglas. 2013. "Truth, Winning, and Simple Determination Pluralism." In *Truth and Pluralism: Current Debates*, edited by Nikolaj J. L. L. Pedersen and Cory D. Wright, 113–122. Oxford, UK: Oxford University Press.

Fallis, Don. 2009. "What Is Lying?" *The Journal of Philosophy* 106 (1):29–56. doi: 10.2307/20620149.

Fallis, Don. 2012. "Davidson Was Almost Right about Lying." *Australasian Journal of Philosophy* 91 (2):337–353. doi: 10.1080/00048402.2012.688980.

Fiss, Owen M. 1982. "Objectivity and Interpretation." *Stanford Law Review* 34 (4):739–763.

Forbes, Graeme. 1994. *Modern Logic: A Text in Elementary Symbolic Logic*. New York: Oxford University Press.

Forster, Paul D. 1996. "The Unity of Peirce's Theories of Truth." *British Journal for the History of Philosophy* 4 (1):119–147. doi: 10.1080/0960878960 8570934.

Foucault, Michel. 1972. *The Archaeology of Knowledge*. London: Tavistock Publications.

Foucault, Michel. 1980. *Power-Knowledge: Selected Interviews and Other Writings, 1972–1977*. Brighton, UK: Harvester Press.

Foucault, Michel. 2002. *The Order of Things: An Archaeology of the Human Sciences*. London: Routledge.

Fricker, Elizabeth. 1994. "Against Gullibility." In *Knowing from Words: Western and Indian Philosophical Analysis of Understanding and Testimony*, edited by B. K. Matilal and A. Chakrabarti, 125–161. The Netherlands: Springer.

Fumerton, Richard. 2013. "Alethic Pluralism and the Correspondence Theory of Truth." In *Truth and Pluralism: Current Debates*, edited by Nikolaj J. L. L. Pedersen and Cory D. Wright, 197–212. Oxford, UK: Oxford University Press.

Gelfert, Axel. 2006. "Kant on Testimony." *British Journal for the History of Philosophy* 14 (4):627–642. doi: 10.1080/09608780600965226.

Giere, Ronald N. 1985. "Constructive Realism." In *Images of Science: Essays on Realism and Empiricism*, edited by Paul M. Churchland and Clifford A. Hooker, 75–98. Chicago: University of Chicago Press.

Gilbert, Margaret. 1989. *On Social Facts*. London: Routledge.

Glanzberg, Michael. 2014. "Truth." In *The Stanford Encyclopedia of Philosophy*, Edward N. Zalta (ed.). Stanford, CA: Stanford University. Accessed February 8, 2016. http://plato.stanford.edu/archives/fall2014/entries/truth.

Glüer, Kathrin, and Åsa Wikforss. 2015. "The Normativity of Meaning and Content." In *The Stanford Encyclopedia of Philosophy*, Edward N. Zalta (ed.). Stanfrod, CA: Stanford University. Accessed February 8, 2016. http://plato.stanford.edu/archives/sum2015/entries/meaning-normativity.

Goldman, Alvin, and Thomas Blanchard. 2015. "Social Epistemology." In *The Stanford Encyclopedia of Philosophy*, Edward N. Zalta (ed.). Stanford, CA: Stanford University. Accessed February 8, 2016. http://plato.stanford.edu/archives/spr2014/entries/grice.

Goodman, Nelson. 1947. "The Problem of Counterfactual Conditionals." *The Journal of Philosophy* 44 (5):113–128. doi: 10.2307/2019988.

Grandy, Richard E., and Richard Warner. 2014. "Paul Grice." In *The Stanford Encyclopedia of Philosophy*, Edward N. Zalta (ed.). Stanford, CA: Stanford University. Accessed February 8, 2016. http://plato.stanford.edu/archives/spr2014/entries/grice.

Grice, Paul. 1989. *Studies in the Way of Words*. Cambridge, MA: Harvard University Press.

Groarke, Leo. 2013. "Informal Logic." In *The Stanford Encyclopedia of Philosophy*, Edward N. Zalta (ed.). Stanford, CA: Stanford University. Accessed February 8, 2016. http.//plato.stanford.edu/archives/sum2015/entries/logic-informal.

Groarke, Leo, and Christopher W. Tindale. 2012. *Good Reasoning Matters! A Constructive Approach to Critical Thinking*. Toronto: Oxford University Press.

Grönroos, Christian. 2011. "Value Co-creation in Service Logic: A Critical Analysis." *Marketing Theory* 11 (3):279–301. doi: 10.1177/1470593111408177.

Grönroos, Christian, and Päivi Voima. 2013. "Critical Service Logic: Making Sense of Value Creation and Co-creation." *Journal of the Academy of Marketing Science* 41 (2):133–150. doi: 10.1007/s11747–012–0308–3.

Guo, Xiaoling, Andy Wei Hao, and Xiaoyan Shang. 2011. "Consumer Perceptions of Brand Functions: An Empirical Study in China." *Journal of Consumer Marketing* 28 (4):269–279. doi: 10.1108/07363761111143169.

Haack, Susan. 1976. "The Pragmatist Theory of Truth." *The British Journal for the Philosophy of Science* 27 (3):231–249. doi: 10.2307/686121.

Haack, Susan. 1993. *Evidence and Inquiry: Towards Reconstruction in Epistemology*. Oxford, UK: Blackwell.

Habermas, Jürgen. 2003. *Truth and Justification*. Translated by Barbara Fultner. Cambridge, MA: MIT Press.

Hansson, Sven Ove. 2007. "The False Dichotomy between Coherentism and Foundationalism." *Journal of Philosophy* 104 (6):290–300. doi: 10.5840/jphil2007104620.

Hayward, Keith, and Majid Yar. 2006. "The 'Chav' Phenomenon: Consumption, Media and the Construction of a New Underclass." *Crime, Media, Culture* 2 (1):9–28. doi: 10.1177/1741659006061708.

Hendricks, Vincent F. 2006. *Mainstream and Formal Epistemology*. New York: Cambridge University Press.

Heneghan, Carl, Rafael Perera, David Nunan, Kamal Mahtani, and Peter Gill. 2012. "Forty Years of Sports Performance Research and Little Insight Gained." 345:e4797. doi: 10.1136/bmj.e4797.

Hookway, Christopher. 2000. *Truth, Rationality and Pragmatism: Themes from Peirce*. Oxford, UK: Oxford University Press.

Hookway, Christopher. 2012. *The Pragmatic Maxim: Essays on Peirce and Pragmatism*. Oxford, UK: Oxford University Press.

Hookway, Christopher. 2015. "Pragmatism." In *The Stanford Encyclopedia of Philosophy*, Edward N. Zalta (ed.). Accessed February 8, 2016. http://plato. stanford.edu/archives/spr2015/entries/pragmatism.

Howat, Andrew. 2014. "Prospects for Peircean Truth." *Canadian Journal of Philosophy* 44 (3–4):365–387. doi: 10.1080/00455091.2014.950473.

Hunt, Shelby D. 1990. "Truth in Marketing Theory and Research." *Journal of Marketing* 54 (3):1–15. doi: 10.2307/1251812.

ICC (International Chamber of Commerce). 2011. Advertising and Marketing Communication Practice: Consolidated ICC Code.

Jackson, Jennifer. 1990. "Honesty in Marketing." *Journal of Applied Philosophy* 7 (1):51–60.

James, William. 1975a. *The Meaning of Truth, The Works of William James*. Cambridge, MA: Harvard University Press.

James, William. 1975b. *Pragmatism, The Works of William James*. Cambridge, MA: Harvard University Press.

Joachim, Harold H. 1939. *The Nature of Truth*. London: Oxford University Press.

Johnston, Mark. 1989. "Dispositional Theories of Value." *Proceedings of the Aristotelian Society, Supplementary Volumes* 63:89–174. doi: 10.2307/4106918.

Joy, Annamma, and Eric Ping Hung Li. 2012. "Studying Consumption Behaviour through Multiple Lenses: An Overview of Consumer Culture Theory." *Journal of Business Anthropology* 1 (1):141–173.

Kant, Immanuel. 2012. *Groundwork of the Metaphysics of Morals*. Translated by Mary Gregor and Jens Timmermann. Cambridge, UK: Cambridge University Press.

Keller, Kevin Lane. 1993. "Conceptualizing, Measuring, and Managing Customer-Based Brand Equity." *Journal of Marketing* 57 (1):1–22. doi: 10.2307/ 1252054.

Keller, Kevin Lane. 2001. Building Customer-Based Brand Equity: A Blueprint for Creating Strong Brands. Cambridge, MA: Marketing Science Institute.

Keller, Kevin Lane. 2008. *Strategic Brand Management*. Upper Saddle River, NJ: Pearson Education.

Keller, Kevin Lane, Brian Sternthal, and Alice Tybout. 2002. "Three Questions You Need to Ask about Your Brand." *Harvard Business Review* (September): 3–8.

Kirkham, Richard L. 1992. *Theories of Truth: A Critical Introduction*. Cambridge, MA: MIT Press.

Kirwan, Christopher. 1971. *Aristotle's Metaphysics*. Oxford, UK: Oxford University Press.

Kitcher, Philip. 2002. "On the Explanatory Role of Correspondence Truth." *Philosophy and Phenomenological Research* 64 (2):346–364. doi: 10.1111/ j.1933–1592.2002.tb00005.x.

Kitcher, Philip. 2004. *Science, Truth and Democracy*. Oxford, UK: Oxford University Press.

Klein, Peter D. 2000. "Contextualism and the Real Nature of Academic Skepticism*." *Philosophical Issues* 10 (1):108–116. doi: 10.1111/j.1758–2237.2000.tb00014.x.

Klement, Kevin. 2015. "Russell's Logical Atomism." In *The Stanford Encyclopedia of Philosophy*, Edward N. Zalta (ed.). Stanford, CA: Stanford University. Accessed February 8, 2016. http://plato.stanford.edu/archives/sum2015/entries/ logical-atomism.

Kornblith, Hilary. 1993. "Epistemic Normativity." *Synthese* 94 (3):357–376. doi: 10.1007/BF01064485.

Kornblith, Hilary (ed.). 1994. *Naturalizing Epistemology*. Cambridge, MA: MIT Press.

Koscholke, Jakob. 2015. "Evaluating Test Cases for Probabilistic Measures of Coherence." *Erkenntnis*: 1–27. doi: 10.1007/s10670–015–9734–1.

Kripke, Saul A. 1982. *Wittgenstein on Rules and Private Language: An Elementary Exposition*. Oxford, UK: Basil Blackwell.

Lebow, Richard Ned. 2004. "Constructive Realism." *International Studies Review* 6 (2):346–348. doi: 10.1111/j.1521–9488.2004.419_5.x.

Lee, Eun-Jung. 2013. "A Prototype of Multicomponent Brand Personality Structure: A Consumption Symbolism Approach." *Psychology & Marketing* 30 (2):173–186. doi: 10.1002/mar.20596.

Legg, Catherine. 2014. "Charles Peirce's Limit Concept of Truth." *Philosophy Compass* 9 (3):204–213. doi: 10.1111/phc3.12114.

Lehrer, Keith. 1990. *Theory of Knowledge*. Boulder, CO.: Westview Press.

Leigh, Thomas W., Cara Peters, and Jeremy Shelton. 2006. "The Consumer Quest for Authenticity: The Multiplicity of Meanings Within the MG Subculture of Consumption." *Journal of the Academy of Marketing Science* 34 (4):481–493. doi: 10.1177/0092070306288403.

Levinson, Stephen C. 2000. *Presumptive Meanings: The Theory of Generalized Conversational Implicature*. Cambridge, MA: MIT Press.

Lewis, Clarence Irving. 1946. *An Analysis of Knowledge and Valuation*. La Salle: Open Court.

Lewis, David. 1969. *Convention: A Philosophical Study*. Cambridge, MA: Harvard University Press.

Lewis, David. 1973. *Counterfactuals*. Oxford, UK: Blackwell.

Lockard, Matthew. 2013. "Epistemic Instrumentalism." *Synthese* 190 (9):1701–1718. doi: 10.1007/s11229–011–9932–6.

López de Sa, Dan. 2010. "The Makings of Truth: Realism, Response-Dependence, and Relativism." In *New Waves in Truth*, edited by Corey D. Wright and Nikolaj J. L. L. Pedersen, 191–204. Basingstoke, UK: Palgrave Macmillan.

Lynch, Michael P. 1998. *Truth in Context*. Cambridge, MA: MIT Press.

Lynch, Michael P. 2004. "Truth and Multiple Realizability." *Australasian Journal of Philosophy* 82 (3):384–408. doi: 10.1080/713659875.

Lynch, Michael P. 2009. *Truth as One and Many*. Oxford, UK: Oxford University Press.

Lynch, Michael P. 2013. "Three Questions for Truth Pluralism." In *Truth and Pluralism*, edited by Nikolaj J. L. L. Pedersen and Cory D. Wright, 21–41. Oxford, UK: Oxford University Press.

Lynch, Michael P. 2015. "Pragmatism and the Price of Truth." In *Meaning Without Representations: Essays on Truth, Expression, Normativity, and Naturalism*, edited by Steven Gross, Nicholas Tebben and Michael Williams, 245–261. Oxford, UK: Oxford University Press.

MacBride, Fraser. 2014. "Truthmakers." In *The Stanford Encyclopedia of Philosophy*, Edward N. Zalta (ed.). Stanford, CA: Stamford University. Accessed February 8, 2016. http://plato.stanford.edu/archives/spr2014/entries/truthmakers.

Marino, Patricia. 2010. "Representation-Friendly Deflationism versus Modest Correspondence." In *New Waves in Truth*, edited by Cory D. Wright and Nikolaj J. L. L. Pedersen, 218–231. New York: Palgrave Macmillan.

McLaughlin, Brian, and Karen Bennett. 2014. "Supervenience." In *The Stanford Encyclopedia of Philosophy*, Edward N. Zalta (ed.). Stanford, CA: Stanford University. Accessed February 8, 2016. http://stanford.edu/archives/spr2014/entries/supervenience.

Misak, Cheryl J. 2013. *The American Pragmatists*. Oxford, UK: Oxford University Press.

Moore, G. E. 1907. Professor James' "Pragmatism." *Proceedings of the Aristotelian Society* 8:33–77. doi: 10.2307/4543758.

Moretti, Luca, and Ken Akiba. 2007. "Probabilistic Measures of Coherence and the Problem of Belief Individuation." *Synthese* 154 (1):73–95. doi: 10.1007/s11229-005-0193-0.

Moynihan, Ray, and Alan Cassels. 2005. *Selling Sickness: How Drug Companies Are Turning Us All into Patients*. Boston: Allen & Unwin.

Moynihan, Ray, Peter C. Gøtzsche, Iona Heath, and David Henry. 2002. "Selling Sickness: The Pharmaceutical Industry and Disease Mongering." *British Medical Journal* 324 (7342):886–891. doi: 10.1136/bmj.324.7342.886.

Niiniluoto, Ilkka. 1998. "Verisimilitude: The Third Period." *The British Journal for the Philosophy of Science* 49 (1):1–29. doi: 10.1093/bjps/49.1.1.

Northcott, Robert. 2013. "Verisimilitude: A Causal Approach." *Synthese* 190 (9):1471–1488. doi: 10.1007/s11229-011-9895-7.

Nottelmann, Nikolaj. 2008. "The Present and Future State of Epistemic Deontologism." In *New Waves in Epistemology*, edited by Vincent F. Hendricks and Duncan Pritchard, 75–105. New York: Palgrave Macmillan.

Nute, Donald. 1975. "Counterfactuals and the Similarity of Words." *The Journal of Philosophy* 72 (21):773–778. doi: 10.2307/2025340.

Oddie, Graham. 2014. "Truthlikeness."In *The Stanford Encyclopedia of Philosophy* Edward N. Zalta (ed.). URL = http://plato.stanford.edu/archives/sum2014/entries/truthlikeness/%3E. Accessed December 9, 2015.

Olshewsky, Thomas M. 1983. "Peirce's Pragmatic Maxim." *Transactions of the Charles S. Peirce Society* 19 (2):199–210. doi: 10.2307/40320008.

Orth, Ulrich R., and Renata De Marchi. 2007. "Understanding the Relationships between Functional, Symbolic, and Experiential Brand Beliefs, Product Experiential Attributes, and Product Schema: Advertising-Trial Interactions Revisited." *The Journal of Marketing Theory and Practice* 15 (3):219–233. doi: 10.2753/MTP1069-6679150303.

Park, C. Whan, Bernard J. Jaworski, and Deborah J. MacInnis. 1986. "Strategic Brand Concept-Image Management." *Journal of Marketing* 50 (4):135–145. doi: 10.2307/1251291.

Pedersen, Nikolaj J. L. L. 2006. "What Can the Problem of Mixed Inferences Teach Us about Alethic Pluralism?" *The Monist*:102–117.

Pedersen, Nikolaj J. L. L. 2012. "Recent Work on Alethic Pluralism." *Analysis* 72 (3):588–607. doi: 10.1093/analys/ans079.

Pedersen, Nikolaj J. 2010. "Stabilizing Alethic Pluralism." *The Philosophical Quarterly* 60 (238):92–108. doi: 10.1111/j.1467–9213.2008.605.x.

Pedersen, Nikolaj J., and Cory D. Wright, eds. 2013. *Truth and Pluralism: Current Debates*. Oxford, UK: Oxford University Press.

Peirce, Charles S. 1986. *Writings of Charles S. Peirce: A Chronological Edition*. Vol. 3. Indianapolis: Indiana University Press.

Plungis, Jeff. 2015. "Carmakers Cheating on Emissions Almost as Old as Pollution Tests." *Bloomberg*, September 23. Accessed December 9, 2015. http://www.bloomberg.com/news/articles/2015-11-17/linkedin-s-hoffman-says-half-of-tech-unicorns-may-not-thrive.

Popper, Karl R. 1976. "A Note on Verisimilitude." *The British Journal for the Philosophy of Science* 27 (2):147–159.

Popper, Karl R. 1963. *Conjectures and Refutations*. London: Routledge.

Popper, Karl R. 1968. *The Logic of Scientific Discovery*. London: Hutchinson.

Popper, Karl R. 1979. *Objective Knowledge: An Evolutionary Approach*. Oxford, UK: Clarendon Press.

Poston, Ted. 2014. *Reason and Explanation: A Defense of Explanatory Coherentism*. Basingstoke, UK: Palgrave Macmillan.

Potter, James W. 2014. *Media Literacy*. Los Angeles, CA: SAGE.

Proops, Ian. 2013. "Wittgenstein's Logical Atomism." In *The Stanford Encyclopedia of Philosophy*, Edward N. Zalta (ed.). Stanford, CA: Stanford University. Accessed February 8, 2016. http://plato.stanford.edu/archives/sum2013/entries/wittgenstein-atomism.

Putnam, Hillary. 1981. *Reason, Truth and History*. Cambridge, UK: Cambridge University Press.

Quine, W. V. O. 1951. "Main Trends in Recent Philosophy: Two Dogmas of Empiricism." *The Philosophical Review* 60 (1):20–43. doi: 10.2307/2181906.

Quine, W. V. O. 2002. "Epistemology Naturalized." In *Knowledge and Inquiry: Readings in Epistemology*, edited by K. Brad Wray, 245–260. Peterborough, Ontario: Broadview Press.

Read, Stephen J., and Amy Marcus-Newhall. 1993. "Explanatory Coherence in Social Explanations: A Parallel Distributed Processing Account." *Journal of Personality and Social Psychology* 65 (3):429–447. doi: 10.1037/0022-3514.65.3.429.

Rescher, Nicholas. 1973. *The Coherence Theory of Truth*. Oxford, UK: Oxford University Press.

Rhodes, R. E., and G-J. de Bruijn. 2013. "How Big Is the Physical Activity Intention-Behaviour Gap? A Meta-Analysis Using the Action Control Framework." *British Journal of Health Psychology* 18 (2):296–309. doi: 10.1111/bjhp.12032.

Rhodes, R. E., and L. Dickau. 2012. "Experimental Evidence for the Intention-Behavior Relationship in the Physical Activity Domain: A Meta-Analysis." *Health Psychology* 31 (6):724–727.

Rindell, Anne. 2013. "Time in Corporate Images: Introducing Image Heritage and Image-in-Use." *Qualitative Market Research: An International Journal* 16 (2):197–213. doi:10.1108/13522751311317594.

Russell, Bertrand. 1992. "William James's Conception of Truth." In *William James: Pragmatism in Focus*, edited by Doris Olin. London: Routledge.

Russell, Bertrand. 1998. *The Problems of Philosophy*. Oxford, UK: Oxford University Press.

Schaffer, Jonathan. 2008a. "Truth and Fundamentality: On Merricks's Truth and Ontology." *Philosophical Books* 49 (4):302–316. doi: 10.1111/j.1468-0149.2008.00470.x.

Schaffer, Jonathan. 2008b. "Truthmaker Commitments." *Philosophical Studies: An International Journal for Philosophy in the Analytic Tradition* 141 (1):7–19. doi: 10.2307/27734312.

Schaffer, Jonathan. 2009. "On What Grounds What." In *Metametaphysics*, edited by D. Chalmers, D. Manley and R. Wasserman, 347–383. Oxford, UK: Oxford University Press.

Schaffer, Jonathan. 2010. "The Least Discerning and Most Promiscuous Truthmaker." *The Philosophical Quarterly* 60 (239):307–324. doi: 10.1111/j.1467-9213.2009.612.x.

Schembri, Sharon, Bill Merrilees, and Stine Kristiansen. 2010. "Brand Consumption and Narrative of the Self." *Psychology and Marketing* 27 (6):623–637. doi: 10.1002/mar.20348.

Schiffer, S. R. 1972. *Meaning*. Oxford, UK: Oxford University Press.

Schippers, Michael. 2014. "Probabilistic Measures of Coherence: from Adequacy Constraints towards Pluralism." *Synthese* 191 (16):3821–3845. doi: 10.1007/s11229-014-0501-7.

Searle, John R. 1969. *Speech Acts: An Essay in the Philosophy of Language*. London: Cambridge University Press.

Sellars, Roy Wood. 1959. "'True' as Contextually Implying Correspondence." *The Journal of Philosophy* 56 (18):717–722. doi: 10.2307/2022183.

Šešelja, Dunja, and Christian Straßer. 2014. "Epistemic Justification in the Context of Pursuit: A Coherentist Approach." *Synthese* 191 (13):3111–3141. doi: 10.1007/s11229-014-0476-4.

Sheeran, Paschal. 2002. "Intention-Behavior Relations: A Conceptual and Empirical Review." *European Review of Social Psychology* 12 (1):1–36. doi: 10.1080/14792772143000003.

Sher, Gila. 2013. "Forms of Correspondence: The Intricate Route from Thought to Reality." In *Truth and Pluralism: Current Debates*, edited by Nikolaj J. L. L. Pedersen and Cory D. Wright, 157–179. Oxford, UK: Oxford University Press.

Shramko, Yaroslav, and Heinrich Wansing. 2015. "Truth Values." In *The Stanford Encyclopedia of Philosophy*, Edward N. Zalta (ed.). Stanford, CA: Stanford University. Accessed February 8, 2016. http://plato.stanford.edu/archives/win2015/entries/truth-values.

Skagestad, Peter. 1981. *The Road of Inquiry: Charles Peirce's Pragmatic Realism*. New York: Columbia University Press.

Sloman, Steven A. 1994. "When Explanations Compete: The Role of Explanatory Coherence on Judgements of Likelihood." *Cognition* 52 (1):1–21. doi: 10.1016/0010-0277(94)90002-7.

Spence, Edward, and Brett van Heekeren. 2005. *Advertising Ethics*. Upper Saddle River, NJ: Pearson Education.

Stalnaker, Robert. 1968. "A Theory of Conditionals." In *Studies in Logical Theory* edited by Nicholas Rescher, 98–112. Oxford, UK: Blackwell.

Stango, Marco. 2015. "The Pragmatic Maxim and the Normative Sciences: Peirce's Problematical 'Fourth' Grade of Clarity." *Transactions of the Charles S. Peirce Society: A Quarterly Journal in American Philosophy* 51 (1):34–56.

Stoljar, Daniel, and Nic Damnjanovic. 2014. "The Deflationary Theory of Truth." In *The Stanford Encyclopedia of Philosophy* Edward N. Zalta (ed.). Stanford,

CA: Stanford University. Accessed February 8, 2016. http://plato.stanford.edu/archives/fall2014/entries/truth-deflationary.

Strawson, Peter F. 1950. "Truth." *Proceedings of the Aristotelian Society, Supplementary Volumes* 24:129–156. doi: 10.2307/4106745.

Sweet, Alec Stone, and Jud Matthews. 2008. "Proportionality Balancing and Global Constitutionalism." *Columbia Journal of Transnational Law* 47 (1):72–164.

Thagard, Paul. 1989. "Explanatory Coherence." *Behavioral and Brain Sciences* 12 (03):435–467. doi: 10.1017/S0140525X00057046.

Thagard, Paul. 2000. *Coherence in Thought and Action.* Cambridge, MA: MIT Press.

Thagard, Paul. 2012. "Coherence: The Price Is Right." *The Southern Journal of Philosophy* 50 (1):42–49. doi: 10.1111/j.2041-6962.2011.00091.x.

van Fraassen, Bas C. 1980. *The Scientific Image.* Oxford, UK: Oxford University Press.

Vargo, Stephen L., and Robert F. Lusch. 2004. "Evolving to a New Dominant Logic for Marketing." *Journal of Marketing* 68 (1):1–17. doi: 10.1509/jmkg.68.1.1.24036.

Veblen, Thorstein. 1899. *The Theory of the Leisure Class.* New York: Macmillan.

Walker, Ralph C. S. 1989. *The Coherence Theory of Truth: Realism, Anti-realism, Idealism.* London: Routledge.

White, Alan R. 1971. *Truth.* London: Macmillan.

Whiting, Daniel. 2007. "The Normativity of Meaning Defended." *Analysis* 67 (2):133–140. doi: 10.1093/analys/67.2.133.

Wiedmann, Klaus-Peter, Nadine Hennigs, Steffen Schmidt, and Thomas Wuestefeld. 2011. "The Importance of Brand Heritage as a Key Performance Driver in Marketing Management." *Journal of Brand Management* 19 (3):182–194.

Williams, Christopher. J. F. 1976. *What Is Truth.* Cambridge, UK: Cambridge University Press.

Wing, Rena R., and Suzanne Phelan. 2005. "Long-Term Weight Loss Maintenance." *The American Journal of Clinical Nutrition* 82 (1):222–225.

Withnall, Adam. 2013. "'Sexist' Skoda Advert Comes under Fire in Ireland." The Independent. Accessed September 9, 2015. http://www.independent.co.uk/news/world/europe/sexist-skoda-advert-comes-under-fire-in-ireland-8901646.html.

Wittgenstein, Ludwig. 1971. *Tractatus Logico-Philosophicus.* London: Routledge & Kegan Paul.

Wright, Cory D. 2005. "On the Functionalization of Pluralist Approaches to Truth." *Synthese* 145 (1):1–28. doi: 10.1007/s11229-004-5863-9.

Wright, Cory D. 2010. "Truth, Ramsification, and the Pluralist's Revenge." *Australasian Journal of Philosophy* 88 (2):265–283. doi: 10.1080/00048400902941315.

Wright, Cory D., and Nikolaj J. L. L Pedersen, eds. 2010a. *New Waves in Truth.* Edited by Vincent F. Hendricks and Duncan Pritchard, *New Waves in Philosophy.* Basingstoke, UK: Palgrave Macmillan.

Wright, Cory D., and Nikolaj J. L. L Pedersen. 2010b. "Truth, Pluralism, Monism, Correspondence." In *New Waves in Truth,* edited by Cory D. Wright and Nikolaj J. L. L Pedersen, 205–217. Basingstoke, UK: Palgrave Macmillan.

Wright, Cory D., and Nikolaj J. L. L. Pedersen. 2010c. "Truth, Pluralism, Monism, Correspondence." In *New Waves in Truth,* edited by Cory D. Wright and Nikolaj J. L. L. Pedersen, 205–217. New York: Palgrave Macmillan.

Wright, Crispin J. G. 1998. "Truth: A Traditional Debate Reviewed." *Canadian Journal of Philosophy* 28 (1):31–74. doi: 10.1080/00455091.1998.10717495.

Wright, Crispin. J. G. 1992. *Truth and Objectivity*. Cambridge, MA: Harvard University Press.

Wright, Crispin. J. G. 1993. *Realism, Meaning and Truth*. Oxford, UK: Oxford University Press.

Wright, Crispin J. G. 2013. "A Plurality of Pluralisms." In *Truth and Pluralism: Current Debates*, edited by Nikolaj J. L. L. Pedersen and Cory D. Wright, 123–153. Oxford, UK: Oxford University Press.

Young, James O. 1995. *Global Anti-realism*. Aldershot, UK: Avebury.

Young, James O. 2001. "A Defence of the Coherence Theory of Truth." *The Journal of Philosophical Research* 26:89–101. doi: 10.5840/jpr_2001_21.

Young, James O. 2015. "The Coherence Theory of Truth." In *Stanford Encyclopedia of Philosophy*, Edward N. Zalta ed.). Stanford, CA: Stanford University. Accessed February 8, 2016. http://plato.stanford.edu/archives/fall2015/entries/truth-coherence.

Zaheer, Srilata, Stuart Albert, and Akbar Zaheer. 1999. "Time Scales and Organizational Theory." *Academy of Management Review* 24 (4):725–741. doi: 10.5465/amr.1999.2553250.

Index

For Product Safety Concerns and Information please contact our EU
representative GPSR@taylorandfrancis.com
Taylor & Francis Verlag GmbH, Kaufingerstraße 24, 80331 München, Germany